AF412078

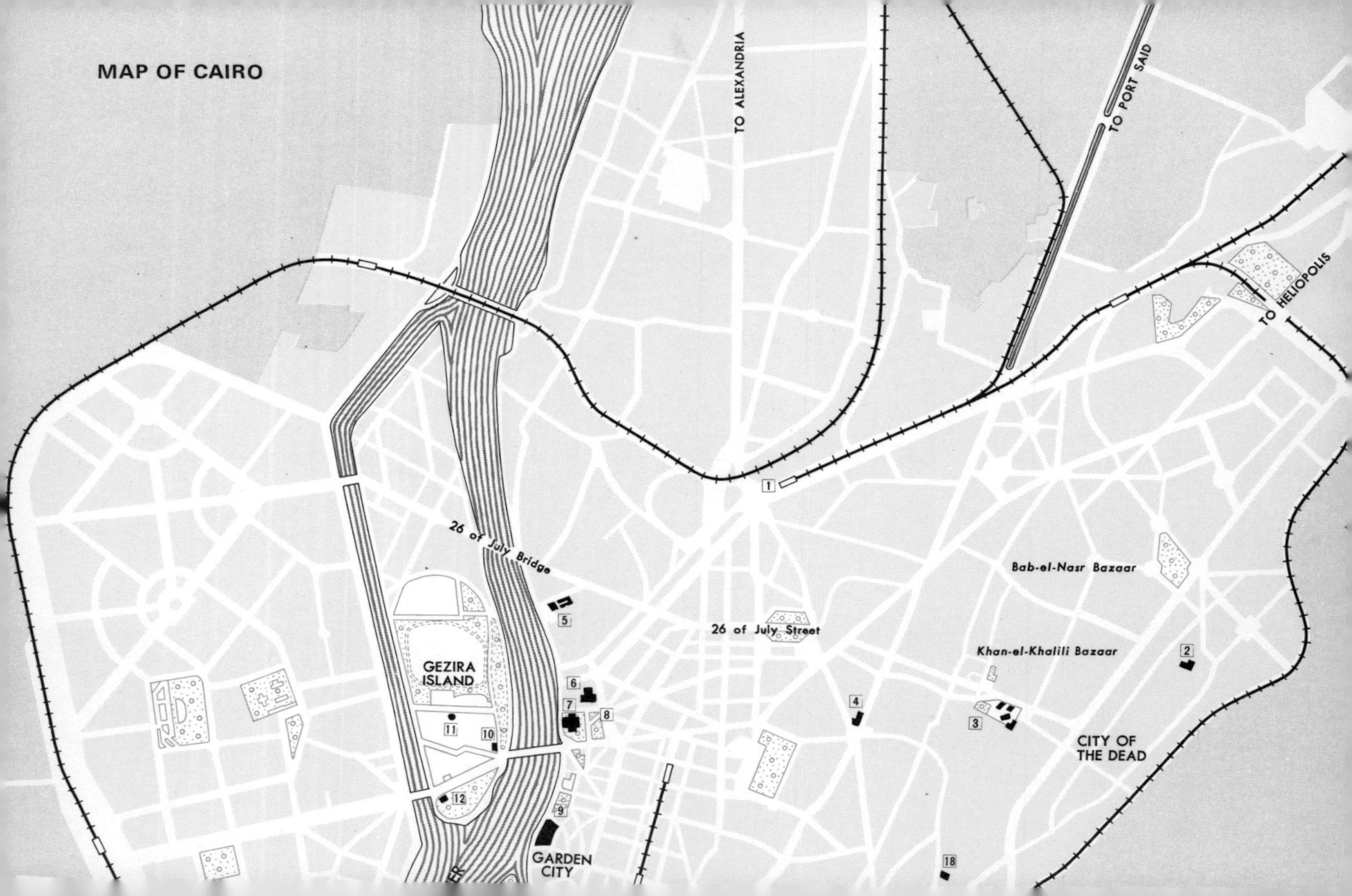

MAP OF CAIRO
TO ALEXANDRIA
TO PORT SAID
TO HELIOPOLIS
26 of July Bridge
26 of July Street
Bab-el-Nasr Bazaar
Khan-el-Khalili Bazaar
GEZIRA ISLAND
GARDEN CITY
CITY OF THE DEAD

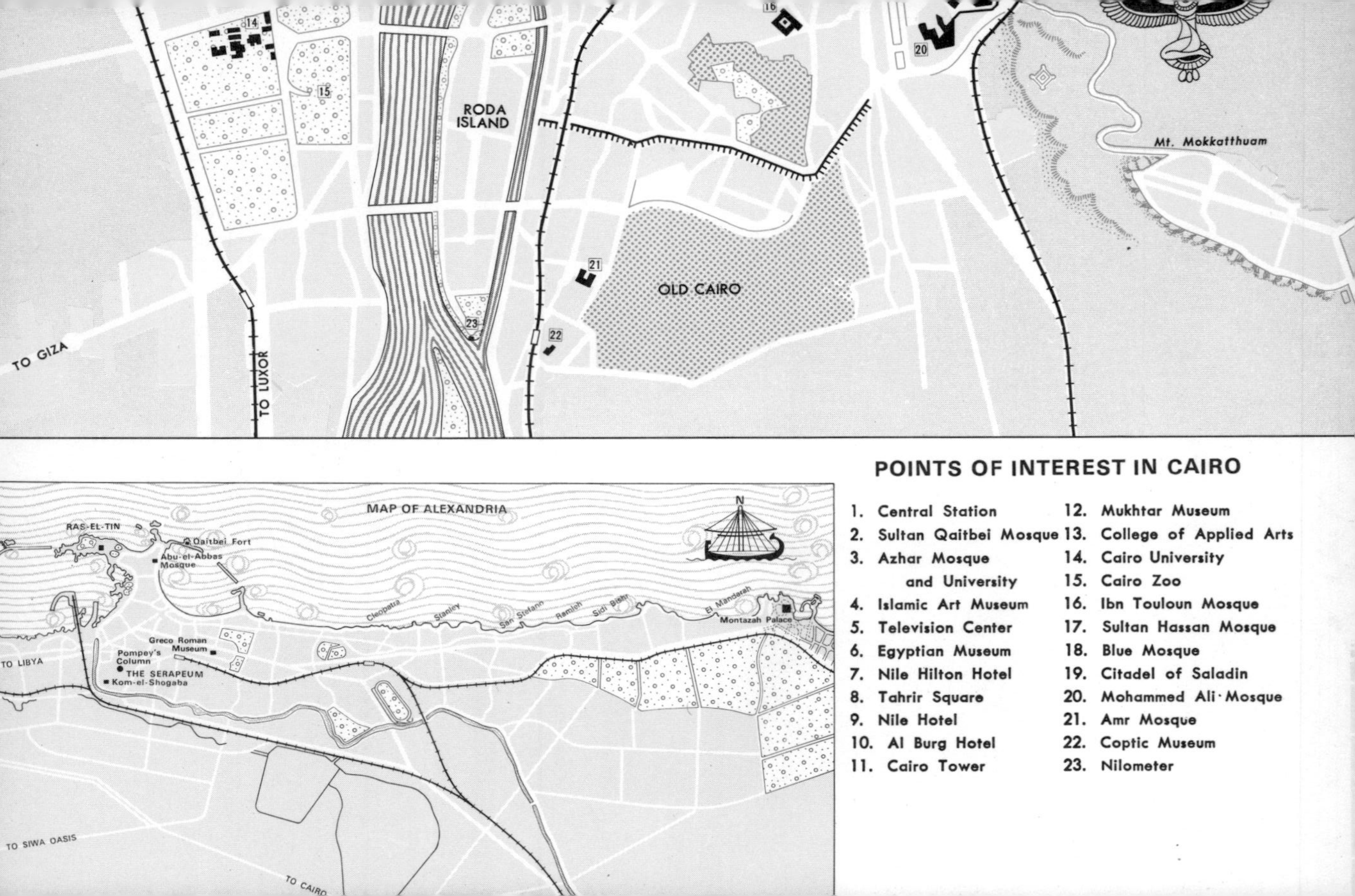

RODA ISLAND
OLD CAIRO
Mt. Mokkatthuam
TO GIZA
TO LUXOR
MAP OF ALEXANDRIA
N
RAS-EL-TIN
Qaitbei Fort
Abu-el-Abbas Mosque
Cleopatra
Stanley
San Stefano
Ramleh
Sidi Bishr
El Mandarah
Montazah Palace
Greco Roman Museum
Pompey's Column
THE SERAPEUM
Kom-el-Shogaba
TO LIBYA
TO SIWA OASIS
TO CAIRO

POINTS OF INTEREST IN CAIRO
1. Central Station
2. Sultan Qaitbei Mosque
3. Azhar Mosque and University
4. Islamic Art Museum
5. Television Center
6. Egyptian Museum
7. Nile Hilton Hotel
8. Tahrir Square
9. Nile Hotel
10. Al Burg Hotel
11. Cairo Tower
12. Mukhtar Museum
13. College of Applied Arts
14. Cairo University
15. Cairo Zoo
16. Ibn Touloun Mosque
17. Sultan Hassan Mosque
18. Blue Mosque
19. Citadel of Saladin
20. Mohammed Ali · Mosque
21. Amr Mosque
22. Coptic Museum
23. Nilometer

Cairo

Feluccas filled with merrymakers after the Ramadan season.

Cairo

NOBUO ASAI
MITSUO NITTA

Translated by Pauline Bush

KODANSHA INTERNATIONAL LTD.
Tokyo, New York & San Francisco

Distributors:

UNITED STATES: *Kodansha International/USA, Ltd. through Harper & Row, Publishers, Inc., 10 East 53rd Street, New York, New York 10022.* SOUTH AMERICA: *Harper & Row, International Department.* CANADA: *Fitzhenry & Whiteside Limited, 150 Lesmill Road, Don Mills, Ontario.* MEXICO AND CENTRAL AMERICA: *HARLA S. A. de C. V., Apartado 30–546, Mexico 4, D. F.* UNITED KINGDOM: *TABS, 7 Maiden Lane, London WC2.* EUROPE: *Boxerbooks Inc., Limmatstrasse 111, 8031 Zurich.* AUSTRALIA AND NEW ZEALAND: *Book Wise (Australia) Pty. Ltd., 104–18 Sussex Street, Sydney.* THAILAND: *Central Department Store Ltd., 306 Silom Road, Bangkok.* HONG KONG AND SINGAPORE: *Books for Asia Ltd., 30 Tat Chee Avenue, Kowloon; 65 Crescent Road, Singapore 15.* THE FAR EAST: *Japan Publications Trading Company, P. O. Box 5030, Tokyo International, Tokyo.*

Published by Kodansha International Ltd., 2–12–21 Otowa, Bunkyo-ku, Tokyo 112 and Kodansha International/USA, Ltd., 10 East 53rd Street, New York, New York 10022 and 44 Montgomery Street, San Francisco, California 94104. Copyright © 1977 by Kodansha International Ltd. All rights reserved. Printed in Japan.

LCC 76–11453
ISBN 0–87011–289–9
JBC 0326–785521–2361

First edition, 1977

Contents

Introduction 7

Cairo 9

The Great Pyramids 75

Alexandria 107

This book is published in collaboration with State Information Service, Cairo, Egypt.

Drawings by Hirobumi Nagakane

Introduction

I am always happy when I am approached to write or talk about Egypt. I am even happier when an overseas friend asks me to introduce a book he has written about my country. And when the friend comes from Japan, then I feel an even greater pleasure because, in spite of the vast distances that separate Egypt and Japan, my country has left impressions strong enough to evoke a whole book.

What is it, then, that makes Egypt so alluring? What kind of magic emanates from Egypt that from time immemorial writers and travelers—Herodotus, Lady Duff Gorden Lane, Comr and a hundred others—have been inspired to write about Egypt and thus have enriched the literature of travel by their efforts.

Perhaps the most apparent characteristic of Egypt is the way everyone is made to feel at home. The moment one sets foot on Egyptian soil, one experiences this typically Egyptian ease and friendliness. Egypt is a land of friendship and love. Every visitor feels that a part of his country, his culture and his civilization can be found in Egypt. And maybe there is. Egypt is the unique possessor of the ability to absorb cultures and civilizations. Invaders have come and gone, armies of occupation have passed through the land. They all discovered that, far from being able to enforce their own norms, they were contained and covered over by the Egyptian culture. But, still, they will find that they have left an imprint that will have become part and parcel of Egyptian life.

Egypt has suffered from biased comments and reports: sometimes the ease of its people is mistaken for laziness, the desire to assist an overseas visitor is misconstrued as interference, the joviality of a policeman is interpreted as shallowness. But after a while the real character of Egypt makes itself known to the visitor and these superficial impressions give way to deeper understanding. It may be that the author plays on some of these superficialities and certain passages may not reflect the real Egypt. Nonetheless, that he has produced this book is in itself proof of the interest Egypt creates in the hearts of her visitors.

Dr. Morsi Saad El-Din
Deputy Minister of Information
Arab Republic of Egypt

Cairo

Africa's Largest City

There is an ancient Egyptian proverb that says "Whoever drinks of the waters of the Nile will return repeatedly." I could not help recalling this saying when, in the spring of 1975, after being gone only a short time, I found myself again visiting the fascinating city of Cairo.

Cairo seemed to demand that I come back. I did not even have much trouble getting through the formalities at the airport, even though Cairo is notorious for its tough immigration procedures. Handing out slightly flamboyant greetings learned from Egyptian friends in my far-from-fluent Arabic, I was through in no time at all. I was so happy to be back that the splendid moustache sported by the authoritative and serious-looking immigration official seemed to my mind more a symbol of friendliness than one of dignity and power.

Once outside the airport terminal, I looked for a taxi. Taxis in Cairo tend to be black with a distinguishing white stripe, and are generally either big Mercedes Benzes or the smaller Fiats. I was looking forward to the comfort of riding in one of the big Mercedes, but here the luck I had had with the immigration authorities ran out, and the only taxi I could find was a small, old jalopy. But it was better than nothing, and somehow, forcing my legs into an area far too small for them, I got in and sank back into the seat.

Unexpectedly, a policeman got into the front passenger seat beside the driver. He was a big fellow, and as he got in I heard the seat groan and watched the taxi fill up. He seemed quite pleased with the prospect of a free lift into town, but I was not at all pleased with the fact that he had said nothing at all to me. With a rage that was probably intensified by the fierce sunlight, my temper began to rise.

"Oh, I take it you're going to pay half the fare!" I demanded, trying to make myself sound as hostile as possible.

"I'm a police officer. I've just come off duty, and I'm on my way home. I live in town and you're going in the same direction, so what difference does it make to you?" was his reasoning. It didn't happen to be mine.

"I hired this taxi, and I have the right to ride in it where I like and how I like!"

"You're already in the taxi, so you're not going to lose anything," he answered. It was clear that this chap had no intention of backing down.

The altercation continued for a few minutes. I was furious, but what could I do?

Suddenly it dawned on me that during the short time I had been away from Cairo I had forgotten how to relax and enjoy myself in this city. In Tokyo or New York, the workings of society are finely tuned. One goes as far as the contract states one should go and no further. In Cairo, the cold, practical approach does not take one far. Cairo society is different. It is down-to-earth, easygoing and sometimes a bit lacking in delicacy. It is as though people here, who have lived close to the harshness of the desert and the historical remains of thousands of years, recognize deep in their hearts how powerless the individual really is. As a result, there is a strong sense of interdependence and the importance of helping one another.

As these thoughts occurred to me, I closed my eyes and resigned myself to the situation. I was definitely back in Cairo. I am certain that the Arabic word *maareish* must have been created for just such an occasion. *Maareish* implies the attitude of "Why worry—it can't be helped—it doesn't matter." *Maareish* has been inbred in the Arabs for at least 1,300 years. If a foreigner in an Arab country does not find and cling to the spirit of *maareish*, he will wind up with frayed nerves and ulcers. As I sat in the taxi, the down-to-earth, common sense atmosphere of Cairo gradually came back to me.

So I paused and muttered *"Maareish"* several times to the police officer and agreed to drop him off at his home. With that the atmosphere in the taxi brightened.

I sat back in the seat, looking out the window. On both sides well-tended palm and eucalyptus trees lined the road. Crowds of Egyptians in long, kaftan-like robes called *galabia* flashed by our vehicle. We reached Cairo Station, with its huge statue of Rameses II, some ten meters tall and weighing sixty-three tons, welcoming visitors to Egypt the way the Statue of Liberty does in New York Harbor.

After a while, we came out onto the banks of the Nile. I must have made this journey from Cairo Airport to the center of the city over a hundred times, but for some reason I always marvel at how nothing seems to change. "It's all just as it was," I thought.

The taxi passed the Nile Hotel, where I had reserved a room, but I purposely said nothing to the driver. When we reached the apartment of the police officer, he got out and, turning to me, pressed me to spend teatime with him. I replied that we would meet some other time, and with the word "*Inshaalah*" (May Allah protect you), I said good-bye to him. With an expansive gesture, he tapped me on the shoulder, confirming, "We're firm friends now," and then he left.

Experiences like this one came to govern all my feelings about this country. A little of the spirit of *maareish* is what has made it possible for me to remember Cairo with such pleasant memories.

Whether the spirits of Cairo were actually demanding my return will never be known, but it was completely by chance that I found myself in Cairo for the second time. I first visited Egypt in September, 1969, at the time of the coup d'état in Libya. I was then chief of my newspaper's New Delhi bureau, but had been assigned to cover the events in Libya, since the Cairo bureau chief was out of the country. I dropped everything and rushed to the Middle East to write about the incident.

When the coup was settled and my work in Libya completed, I headed back to New Delhi, stopping in Cairo for a few days. Thinking this was likely to be my only opportunity to visit Egypt, I played the part of the insatiable tourist, traveling everywhere and seeing all there was to see.

But soon after my holiday in Cairo, to my astonishment and pleasure, I was sent to head our bureau there. Since my posting to Cairo, which lasted a little over three years, I have returned to Egypt a number of times. I suppose it would be true to say that it was my business to get to know life in the Middle East as well as I could. From the development of my career since 1969, it would in a sense be true to say that Colonel Gaddafi's take over was a fateful event, not only for Libya, but also for me.

There is little real similarity between the Illinois town built at the confluence of the Mississippi and Ohio rivers and the Arabian city after which it was named. It seems that some American pioneers were reminded of the ancient Egyptian city on the Nile, its water running out into a delta, when they saw the place where the two great American rivers join together to form a watery fan. Apparently, on the basis of this superficial geographical resemblance, the American city was named Cairo. So other than the name itself and the fact that the cities stand beside wide rivers, there is no parallel to be drawn between Cairo, Illinois, and the original Cairo.

I think there are three things which impress themselves forcefully on the first-time visitor to Cairo—a certain pungent odor, the dryness of the atmosphere and the noise.

Visitors arriving in Cairo by plane who are not used to the sounds and smells of the Middle East are likely to be struck by the heavy, cloying odor which permeates the airport buildings. It seems to be the smell of lamb, mixed with the odor of coconut oil.

Lamb is consumed in huge quantities in Egypt, as it is throughout the Arab world. So much so that the word "meat" is automatically assumed to mean "lamb." At festival times, butchers' stalls at the Ataba Bazaar sag under mountains of sheeps' heads, brains, stomachs, offal and legs tied in bundles. Three-wheeled trucks laden with meat race through the streets of the capital. Driving around Cairo, I often found myself behind one of those vehicles piled high with whole carcasses of sheep. The heads would still be on and the eyes open. This could be most disconcerting, and I was frequently startled at the animate way those eyes stared at me.

Anyone who does not like the smell of mutton is bound to grimace on landing at Cairo Airport. But like it or not, this is one of the things most people recall about the city and that gives me the feeling of coming home, of really being back in Cairo.

The supreme dish to lamb gourmets is a whole roast, and the eyes are considered the greatest delicacy. Naturally, they go to the guest of honor. I had them presented to me once. I found them gristly and lacking in flavor until I bit into them. . . .

Winter is the best time of the year in Cairo. It starts in November and the dry, refreshing winter air usually lasts until March. Winter is followed by the Khamshin season, "khamshin" being the Arabic word for "fifty." It is called this because frequent sandstorms scour the city during this fifty-day period. The sand colors the sky ochre and a fine yellow dust hangs in the air, covering everything, getting everywhere. The sand gets into one's ears, nose and pores. Even the precaution of keeping doors and windows closed during this hot season does not prevent the sand from sifting into the house, and filtering into clothes shut up in wardrobes and closets. Landing at Cairo Airport during Khamshin, one gets the impression that the city is at the bottom of a yellow lake. When Khamshin conditions are too bad, flights are cancelled.

The air in Cairo tends to be dry all year, and everything becomes dehydrated as the water in the atmosphere evaporates. One's throat seems to be permanently dry. As a result, whenever friends call on each other in Egypt, the host immediately offers his guest coffee or tea. If coffee, it will be the thick Egyptian coffee known as "*ahwa*". The heavy dregs of *ahwa* sink to the bottom of the cup and one drinks only the liquid that floats on top. Not only do coffee and tea soothe a parched throat, they also help replace some of the body's continuously evaporating water.

Coffee and tea drinking is a serious business in this desert city, so conversation does not begin until they have been consumed. Then the well-bred Egyptian guest asks his host a multitude of questions in rapid succession. The questions generally cover the state of his host's health, what his wife is doing nowadays, whether his children are taking their schoolwork seriously, if his hens are laying and so on. This kindly interrogation is an extremely important factor in establishing friendly relations in Egypt. It is one's duty as a friend to make pleasant conversation over a cup of coffee or tea. And when the last of the coffee is drunk, there is the chance for even more chatting as the coffee grounds, like tea leaves, supposedly indicate the future. Coffee and tea are not just thirst-quenching drinks, they mean much more. In Egypt, they are the lubricants which keep the wheels of human relationships rolling smoothly.

The dry climate creates extremes of temperatures. Temperatures rise quickly during the daytime, and fall with equal rapidity after sundown. It can become suprisingly cold in the evenings, so it usually is necessary to wear extra clothing.

Each day dawns fine and bright. Because the weather is consistently good, it seldom becomes a topic of conversation—except on those rare days when it rains, and then quite a commotion is made about it.

I recall an incident that occurred when I was rushing by taxi to the airport to catch my plane. It started to rain, and because there are no drainage ditches in the roads in Cairo, the road to the airport soon was flooded. I shut the car window against the downpour, but the rain found a crack and began to seep in. Before long, water had gotten into the engine, and the taxi came to a sloshing halt. All I could think about was missing my flight.

The driver got out, propped up the hood and began mopping the rain water with a rag, puffing his cheeks out as he did to blow the raindrops away.

"This must be a real old junk heap if a drop of rain puts the engine out of order," I growled. Worried about making it to the airport in time I thoughtlessly began to be abusive. But the driver took it all in stride and replied, in all seriousness, that I was mistaken. There was nothing wrong with the car. It was the rain that was causing all the trouble.

Even now I have to smile when I remember the driver's explanation. Rainfall is something Egyptians do not really understand. Their lives and their awareness have become attuned, over thousands of years, to clear skies and dry weather. I know of no shop in Cairo where it is possible to purchase an umbrella or overshoes, although every third shop sells either clothes or shoes.

The clothing stores overflow with goods made of Egyptian cotton, the finest cotton in the world, and tourists frequently buy Egyptian cotton shirts to take home as presents or souvenirs. Egyptian-made leather shoes, however, are not in the same category. At first glance they appear to be well made, but the moment they get wet, they start to fall apart. They seem to be made only of leather and glue, and only for fair weather.

No one carries an umbrella in Egypt, and anyone who does is the object of curious glances. When it rains in Egypt, the thing to do is to stay indoors. Everyone is so used to the weather being fine, that their only reaction is to wait for the sky to clear up.

However, there are more clouds in the sky than there used to be, and the number of rainy days is increasing. Some blame the increased humidity on the Aswan High Dam. The completion of the dam increased irrigation facilities for the fertile land around the Nile. The additional surface area of water in the region means that more evaporation takes place and the extra water vapor created in the atmosphere forms clouds.

The increased humidity has already begun to affect life in Egypt. A major problem that has arisen is the preservation of the country's ancient monuments and excavated relics which are of such great historical importance to Eygpt and the rest of the world. Some believe that the more humid conditions will intensify their erosion and that the monuments, which have been preserved for thousands of years by the dry climate, will crumble away. One step that has already been taken to preserve the valuable information yielded by the country's ancient monuments has been the establishment of the Documents Center within the Ministry of Culture for the specific purpose of gathering and cataloguing material on Egyptian relics.

A good starting place to collect data on ancient Egypt is the Egypt Museum in Cairo, generally recognized as one of the greatest storehouses of relics in the world. But even here the effects of the rising humidity are beginning to manifest themselves, so museum officials have started to measure and check the humidity of the building's interior. A visit to the Mummies Section in the southwest corner of the first floor is a fascinating, although rather eerie, experience. Mummies which were buried thousands of years ago, their skins a dark walnut brown, are displayed here. Although they have survived many ages, in recent decades bacteria, insects and fungi have begun to attack them. Consequently, the humidity in the room where they are kept is now being strictly controlled and hygrometers have been placed at several places on the walls.

Probably the most important mummy, that of Rameses II, has suffered the most damage. Consequently, in 1976 Rameses was flown to Paris to be restored by experts there.

In the northwest corner of the same floor is a glass display case containing scarabs that date back to the age of the Pharaohs, but now the mildew seems to be attacking them too. The scarab is a seal patterned after the shape of the dung beetle. The most ancient of Egyptian peoples thought the dung beetle laid its eggs in the little balls of dung it collected. They viewed this as representative of the life cycle and the durability of the human soul. They would place these seals or amulets made out of beetles—in later eras, they were carved of stone instead—in the eyes, ears and nose of the dead at the time of burial to ward off evil.

Today modern scarabs, which are often made of semiprecious stones and are usually a cloudy beige or fresh green in color, are fashioned into rings and pendants to be sold in the bazaars. Besides having traditionally served as amulets for the dead, and now as jewels for women, they have also appeared in at least one book. In the mystery thriller *The Scarab Murder Case* by S. S. Van Dine, a scarab thrown beside the dead body was the clue to who committed the murder.

It is very strange to find mildew in Egypt because the dry climate is not conducive to the reproduction of bacteria. Therefore contagious diseases do not flourish and epidemics are surprisingly rare. The main illness that plagues foreigners is the tummy upset we all seem to have during the first week of our stay, but this is due to the difference in the drinking water. Apparently Egyptians traveling abroad have a similar experience as they too are affected by drinking water they are not used to.

This is not to say that Egypt is completely free of epidemics. In fact, during my stay in Cairo, I heard that there had been a massive outbreak of cholera. I was then living in a rented apartment, and my maid urged me to get myself innoculated. From time to time a white van, which looked like an ambulance, would drive through the streets, spraying the air with a disinfectant which floated out like billows of white smoke. According to an aquaintance, who is a doctor with the World Health Organization in Cairo, it seemed that some 500 people had caught cholera, but the government had not announced it. Since the newspapers carried no mention of this, I assumed they did not consider it newsworthy. Eventually someone asked about it at one of our regular press conferences at the Ministry of Information. The government spokesman casually answered the question, commenting that the story of an epidemic was "probably a rumor that had been spread as part of Israel's psychological warfare." One American journalist standing next to me shrugged his shoulders and mumbled something about "these Egyptians living in a fantasy world. . . ."

As it turned out, the Egyptians were not unknowingly living in a fantasy world. At that time, it was government policy not to disclose any information on any matter that was inconvenient or likely to be a source of shame or embarrassment to the country. Any item of news not officially announced by the authorities was banned from publication.

Sometimes it was frustrating for foreign newsmen, and a number of them made a break to the more liberal climate of Beirut. But journalists engaged on their mini-exodus would only receive a smile from the officials at the Ministry of Information, who would nod and say, "You will return to the Nile." Or they might mutter the oft-quoted words of the celebrated explorer of the desert, Ahmad Hassanein, "The desert is harsh and severe, but once you have known it, you will always return." And the reporters usually did.

Then in 1973 there came a change, probably the result of the success of Egypt's campaign for the possession of the Suez Canal. President Sadat announced that it was time the Egyptian people were made aware of the facts "even if they are sometimes painful." The news climate relaxed considerably; it finally was possible to buy copies of American magazines such as *Time* and *Newsweek* even if some stories were critical of Egypt. Prior to this, these publications had been banned by the authorities.

Along with the smell and the exceptional weather, the third element that gives one the true feeling of Cairo is NOISE! The city is a cacophony of varied and unceasing sounds. The solemn tones of the Koran being chanted and voices raised in prayer are not merely empty forms of religious ritual, they are an important thread in the fabric of life in Egypt, both public and private. The May Day Celebrations and the National Assembly open with the chanting of the Koran and the offering of prayers to Allah. Then President Sadat delivers his opening speech. Speaking intensely in his distinct persuasive voice, his remarks are full of force: "The words of the Soviet Union have proved false. . . . They promise weapons but send none."

Not only in Cairo but throughout the Islamic world it is not unusual to be awakened in the morning by the sound of a sonorous wailing male voice from the next room. Someone is chanting the Koran. In my travels through the Middle East I have frequently been awakened by this chant. I always imagined that the voice belonged to an old man, his white hair giving him the semblance of a holy man, kneeling on the floor, facing Mecca and solemnly reciting his prayers. But bumping into my next-door neighbor on the way to breakfast, I was often surprised to find that the owner of the voice was a young man in his late teens or early twenties, carrying an attaché case and enveloped in the scent of cologne. I would be slightly taken aback at the sound of his cheery "Good morning," proffered in a somewhat high-pitched voice.

One of the unforgettable sounds of Egypt is the voice of the muezzin at dawn and sunset, solemnly calling the faithful to prayer. The voice is loud and resonant, and while it reverberates over the city the barking of the dogs and the cries of birds seem to be stilled. Even nonbelievers hearing the voice of the muezzin feel impelled to stand still, close their eyes and pray.

The position of muezzin is hereditary, and boys start to receive voice training at a very early age. The muezzin of the Azhar

Mosque, one of the oldest and most famed mosques in Cairo, enjoys a high social standing.

When it isn't praying, Cairo is a noisy, bustling city. With the rapid increase in the influx of people from the rural areas, Cairo has suddenly become a major world capital with a population of around eight million. The rise in the urban population has been accompanied by an equally dramatic increase in the number of automobiles. For example, in the late afternoon a steady stream of cars moves along the busy roads radiating like spokes from the city's hub, Talaat Harb Square—a place I prefer to call by its old name of Soliman Pacha Square. Suddenly there will be a screech of brakes and the flow of traffic will come to a halt to the accompaniment of a terrifying number of horns honking and the loud voices of drivers hurling abuses at one another. The windows of the automobiles are open, with the car radios blaring at full volume Arab music to the monotonous beat of the tambourine. Sitting in my car in the sweltering heat, I would soon join the chorus of yellers telling the world to get moving, almost without realizing I was doing so.

The concept of noise pollution, or the idea of blasting horns being an infringement of the public's right to quiet, is nonexistent in Cairo. If anything, the opposite is true. There is a feeling that each individual has to make his or her own contribution to the general noise, as though the number of decibels is still insufficient. Everyone and everything is involved.

Despite the recent growth in the number of automobiles, the donkey still remains an important means of transportation in Cairo. Gentle beasts, their heads bent slightly forward and their long eyelashes pointed modestly to the ground, they seem capable of carrying loads many times their own weight. "*Homar*," the Arabic word for donkey also has the meaning of "idiot." While, personally, I am loathe to think of them that way, I must admit that a donkey's foolish-sounding and high-pitched "hee-haw," which can easily grate on one's nerves, is extremely idiotic.

And when an Egyptian is speaking on the telephone, it is quite easy to hear what the person on the other end of the line is saying. They YELL to each other over the line. It does not matter if they hold the receiver in a normal way or if they hold the receiver six inches away, they YELL!

The fact that sound does not carry easily in the boundless wastes of the desert may be one reason why Egyptians insist on being so loud. Speaking quietly is ineffectual, and therefore loud voices are cultivated naturally. I do not know if this explanation is true , but it seems plausible.

Not only do people here have loud voices, they are also emotional, and the Arabic language is one that appeals strongly to the emotions. The night before the revolution in 1952, Nasser is said to have addressed his fellow revolutionaries in English, urging them to remain calm during the forthcoming upheaval. Asked why he had chosen to speak in English on such an important occasion, Nasser explained, "The Arabic language possesses no words to express the idea of calm."

The hundreds of first-time visitors I have taken around Cairo are usually most impressed by two places in particular. Their emotions are first touched as they enter the city and come out onto the banks of the Nile, traveling along the road from the airport. And many have had their breath taken away when they first see one of the Great Pyramids. They are finally seeing with their own eyes something they have been told about all their lives. At last they can confirm the actual existence of something which was no more than a shadow in their minds before.

Viewed from above, the desert stretches out in all directions, the color of café au lait, divided only by the Nile, a blue ribbon running in an almost straight line across the country from north to south. Some say that since the completion of the Aswan High Dam, the waters of the Nile have become much clearer, and many think that the fertile loam which used to be carried down to the Delta from the upper reaches of the river is now trapped by the dam.

Where the Nile passes through central Cairo, two famous islands rise out of the river, resembling a pair of floating battle-ships. These are the islands of Gezira, in the north, and Roda, in the south. By tradition, long-time foreign residents of Cairo live in the expensive and luxurious apartments surrounded by trees in the Zamalek district on the island of Gezira. I was fortunate to find an apartment in this district and I rented it for the time I was living in Cairo. One of the visitors I entertained in my apartment was worried that if the area was flooded when the waters of the Nile rose I might drown. I was able to assure him that, unlike the time of the Pharaohs, the amount of water carried down by the Nile is now strictly controlled.

In the center of Gezira Island is a fully equipped sports club which includes golf links, a racetrack, a swimming pool and football field. The racetrack's fame escalated when the cover of the Israeli spy Wolfgang Lotz was broken. Masquerading as a racehorse breeder from West Germany, Lotz came and went freely to the racecourse, becoming an intimate of high-ranking politicans and army officers. Living a life as luxurious as that of a James Bond, he was dubbed the "Champagne Spy."

Standing at the southern edge of the Sports Club is the Cairo Tower, built, so it is said, with funds from the U.S. Central Intelligence Agency. The money was apparently given to Nasser, who felt it should be used for the country, so he had the tower built. The story is that the CIA secretly built a device at the base of the tower which would have enabled them to blow it up from a ship in the Mediterranean by remote control. When Nasser made his proclamation nationalizing the Suez Canal, John Foster Dulles, then U.S. secretary of state, allegedly ordered the tower be blown up, but before the order could be carried out, Nasser's intelligence officers discovered the device and disarmed it. As a result, the tower is still standing. From the observatory on the roof it is possible to see all of Cairo spread out below, and to look right across to the Great Pyramids. From the tower's height, the great width of the Nile flowing past becomes apparent.

Two bridges link Gezira Island to the east bank of the Nile, where the government ministries and other municipal buildings are located. The northern bridge, which gives its name to the road it carries, is called the 26 of July Bridge. It was given the name in 1952, in commemoration of the day when King Farouk signed his abdication, marking the success of the Republican Revolution. On the same day, four years later, Nasser nationalized the Suez Canal, so that the date has a special significance for Egyptian nationalism. The southern bridge, its approaches guarded by four stone lions, has a name that is also connected with the revolution. Liberation Bridge is crossed by a road of the same name which passes by the Hilton Hotel where it looks out over Tahrir Square. The names of both bridges seem to reflect the deep political consideration of the leaders of the time, because each of them carries one of the two trunk roads of Cairo.

The conglomeration of skyscapers on the east bank of the Nile, which were built following the revolution, are popularly known as "Nasser's Pyramids." At the northern end of the complex is Television Center, a huge, cylindrical building. Not far from it is the headquarters of the most powerful political party in Egypt, the Arab Socialist Union, as well as the Hilton Hotel and the head office of the Arab League. During the time of the British occupation of Egypt, British troops were garrisoned in this area. Strategically positioned, they could close the bridges immediately at the first sign of unrest among the Egyptians and protect the civilians living in the foreign quarter of Gezira Island.

Television Center contains not only transmission centers for both radio and television, but also the Ministry of Information and the Press Center, the haunt of resident and visiting foreign journalists alike. During my stay in Cairo, I drove to the Press Center everyday from my apartment in Zamalek.

For some time after my arrival, the Israeli Air Force was still making air raids in the area around Cairo. The residential quarter of Cairo, the Maadi, is situated in the south. When the Maadi was being attacked, the glass in the windows of my apartment shook and rattled ominously. For a while the noise of the traffic would die down, and the silence that usually accompanied the hottest part of the afternoon would reign. The camels would sit out the attack at the side of the road, their bodies neatly compact, their long legs folded under them and their eyes tightly shut. I can remember often watching them, completely fascinated.

A frequent topic of conversation at the Press Center during that time was how to cross the Nile from the island if the bridges were attacked. Someone came up with the idea of chartering a boat. But this worry was like comments on rainy weather, everyone talked about it, but nobody would do anything about it.

The Nile is a photogenic river. I once attempted to take a picture of the feluccas, the traditional boats of the Nile, with their distinctive triangular sails, from the first-floor balcony of Television Center. I was using a telescopic lens which captured the feluccas and the people strolling along the banks of the Nile or gazing over the parapets into the water in the foreground. I had the apartment blocks of Zamalek with their rows of palm trees and Cairo Tower in the background. Unfortunately, before I snapped the shutter, an officer from the Ministry of Information reached for the camera and quietly asked me why I was trying to take a picture of the two bridges. The bridges are regarded as military installations. Both are fitted with antimine devices around their girders. At that time, armed soldiers patrolled their approaches, and others were bivouacked in the vicinity of the bridges.

I found it difficult to believe that I was threatening the safety of the bridges by taking a picture with them in it. I explained my intention and the fact that the bridges had not been the object of the photograph. The officer seemed to understand at once.

As there had been no one near me when I was lining up my shot, I can only assume that someone in the distance had spotted me and reported me to the authorities. The secret police are extremely powerful in Cairo and are particularly vigilant around hotel lobbies and shopping areas, places which are frequented by visitors. One could not be blamed for regarding waiters in restaurants, shoeshine boys, maids, porters or taxi drivers as possible secret agents.

A few days after this incident with the photograph, I saw a female tourist have her picture taken with a smiling soldier, right beside the bridge. I didn't know what to think. Had the security measures been relaxed suddenly, or was it just a case of the Egyptian soldiers having a soft spot for a pretty girl?

Generally speaking, Egyptian children are fascinated by cameras, and if you happen to be carrying one they will immediately gather around you. Adults, on the other hand, are extremely cautious. This may have some connection with the fact that the painting of human images is forbidden by the law of Islam, but it is also apparent that many of them feel that something is being snatched from them if someone snaps their picture. Once, when I had taken the photograph of one of the waiters in the dining car of the train on the way to Aswan, my subject told me very sharply that I had "injured his face and would have to pay him compensation."

The heart of "Nasser's Pyramids" is probably the Hilton Hotel. Nasser himself laid the foundation stone. The blue of the hotel makes it a focal point in a sea of yellowish buildings which reflect the colors of the desert. Whether or not it is because most Arabs live in a dry world of sand and dust that they thirst for water and vegetation, I am unable to judge, but Arabs must like blues and greens because those two colors predominate the flags of most Arab nations. Even when a blackout was imposed in Cairo, the color black was not used. Instead the headlights of cars and the windows of buildings were painted dark green or blue.

Arabs have traditionally preferred dark colors, but recently buildings constructed in the Zamalek and Doqqi residential areas have sand-colored or white walls; hotel buildings may be painted a light blue. I can only assume this is the result of a change in aesthetic standards.

The Hilton Hotel faces the Nile, and the rooms on the western side, those with a view of the Great Pyramids, are known as the "Riverside Rooms." They are slightly more expensive than the rooms overlooking Liberation Square on the east. When the hotel is being used for large political conferences, which is very frequently, other guests are quickly moved out.

During the September conference of Arab heads of state, who met in 1970 to try to resolve the civil war in Jordan, Gamal Abdel Nasser stayed on the twelfth floor of the hotel. According to a famous Egyptian journalist, Hassanein Heikal, Nasser is supposed to have remarked that it was like being housed in a barracks. Nevertheless, when the late President was ready for lunch he ordered only a Gruyere cheese sandwich. Heikal told Nasser that in his place he would have ordered smoked-salmon canapés and a dry martini. Nasser responded by asking him if he didn't think that he would go to hell as punishment for drinking strong liquor. Although Islamic law forbids the drinking of alcohol, rules have relaxed a little and quite a variety of alcoholic beverages are produced in Egypt. But Islam's rigid rules are still important, and I believe that Nasser was speaking from the bottom of his heart when he made the remark.

The conference successfully drew up a plan to end the conflict, but, just as the meeting was to close, on September 28 Nasser was stricken by a heart attack and died. Nasser was passionately fond of Gruyère cheese, but because cheese is high in fat, he had been forbidden to eat it by his doctor. The cheese sandwich that the reporter had slighted was the last delicacy Nasser enjoyed.

On the day of his funeral, Nasser's body was transferred from the Revolutionary Council on Gezira Island, where he had lain in state, across Liberation Bridge and from there onto Corniche Road. The weight of the crowds who rushed down to touch the coffin was so great that there was a serious danger of the bridge collapsing. Nasser was buried in Nasser Mosque at Heliopolis, near the airport.

While he was alive, Nasser had said he wanted to present the people of Cairo with a new mosque, and one was designed and built according to his specifications. It is quite likely that he never imagined he would be laid to rest there and that the mosque would eventually be named after him. There are so many mosques in Cairo that more than 1,000 minarets reach up to the sky, but the Nasser Mosque has become established as one of the more popular sightseeing spots.

Religious precedent precludes foreign women from entering mosques without special permission. There is no argument that the position of women throughout the Islamic world is low. The Koran contains the statement: "Since God made men superior to women, men should rule women in all things." As long as Muslims remain devoted in an unchanging way to the teachings of the Koran, there is no possibility of the positions of men and women becoming equal. This being so, women's virtue is highly prized. As one female Egyptian sociologist says, "A woman's virtue is valued for itself. Families always worry that their daughters might commit an indiscretion and bring shame to their house."

During my stay in Egypt, I had the opportunity of meeting Ms. A. Said, editor-in-chief of the influential women's weekly *Al Hawa* and one of Egypt's strongest advocates of the women's movement. Thirty years ago she was the first female student to enter Cairo University. Recalling her days as an undergraduate, she told me that she had eggs thrown at her while she was playing tennis because her arms and legs were exposed. Today, educated women in Egypt have strong ideas about women's rights. Sekina Sadat, a journalist and a daughter of President Sadat, visited Japan; she told me she strongly resented it when, at a sukiyaki party she attended, the Japanese hostesses served the men first. She believes that women in Japan are not treated fairly.

Generally speaking, it is difficult for young Egyptian men to mingle with young women. However, a visit to the departure lounge of Cairo International Airport or Cairo Central Station can be quite startling. Men and women—as well as men and men, and women and women—embrace and kiss each other repeatedly. For foreigners unaccustomed to seeing men hugging each other so enthusiastically, it is a bizarre sight.

But bizarreness aside, the magazine *Sabah-el-Khayr* revealed that some of the heterosexual couples publically displaying their affection are not travelers. The magazine explained, "Since they would be arrested if they were seen kissing in the center of town, young couples pick up a suitcase and make for either the Central Station or the airport."

The Middle East would not be the same without its belly dancers, but in a region where it is thought unsuitable for women to expose their bodies, it is easy to see that belly dancing is definitely not considered a genteel occupation. Nevertheless, belly dancers perform in most of the big hotels and nightclubs in Cairo. I have seen many of them, but my favorite was Nagwa Fouad.

Nagwa Fouad was the regular dancer at the Al-Hambra nightclub in the Sheraton Hotel. My preference for Nagwa was supported by the fact that she was also the favorite of the great majority of Egyptians who considered her to be the top belly dancer in Cairo. The symmetrical beauty of her dance held the audience spellbound, as if she had caught them in a spider's web and there they hung helpless.

A Palestinian by birth, she left her homeland during the Palestinian War. She lived in Beirut until her father discovered she had been secretly taking ballet lessons. He disowned her and she moved to Cairo. She heard favorable reports about belly dancing and decided to try to make a career out of it. It was a good decision because she was an immediate hit. Twelve years later, when she was reunited with her father for the first time since she had left Beirut, he was the first to break down and weep, confessing, "I couldn't wait to see you any longer." It is said that after thirty years of dancing, the soles of her feet have been worn completely smooth.

Belly dancers seem to lead sad lives. In the past they were the playthings of the influential, and now they are showpieces for wealthy Egyptians and overseas visitors. They are made of stern stuff, but they still have an aura of sadness about them.

I managed to make an appointment for an interview with Nagwa Fouad towards the end of November,1971. I was to have met her after her performance, but on the afternoon of the same day, Wasfi Tal, the Jordanian prime minister, was assassinated by a Palestinian in the main lobby of the Sheraton Hotel, where his blood sank into the carpet leaving a brownish red stain. The show for that evening at the Al-Hambra was cancelled. A few days later, I flew out of Cairo to cover the outbreak of the Indo-Pakistan War and remained out of Egypt for two months. I was never able to reschedule my interview with Nagwa Fouad and I shall always regret not having heard the story of her life from her own lips.

The other woman I regret not having met is Madame Gaddafi, wife of the President of Libya. On the opposite bank of the Nile, directly across from the Sheraton, is the Semiramis Hotel. The Semiramis takes its name from the queen in the Assyrian and Babylonian legend who is said to have created the Hanging Gardens of Babylon, one of the Seven Wonders of the Ancient World. When I heard that the wife of Colonel Gaddafi, chairman of the Libyan Revolutionary Council, was to cut the tape marking the opening of an exhibition to be held at the hotel, I dropped what I was doing, grabbed my camera and rushed over to the Semiramis. Waiting in the lobby for the chance to get a picture of her, I was approached by a man who appeared to be a plain-clothes security officer, and was asked not to take any photographs. "Madame Gaddafi does not wish to be photo-graphed," he explained. He added that an interview with her would be out of the question. Madame Gaddafi's reluctance to have her photograph taken was no doubt due to Libya's strict adherence to Islam. Without my photograph and without the chance of an interview, all I was able to do was to catch a glimpse of the hem of her long yellow dress, decorated with a black and brown motif, fluttering in the breeze as she passed in front of me, leaving a slight perfume lingering in the air behind her.

The Semiramis is an old-style hotel. According to one of the guidebooks published by the Tourist Development Association of Egypt, it opened in 1934. The guidebook contains photographs of members of the royal houses and nobility of Europe who stayed there. Recently it has become the haunt of writers. At one time Mahmud Darwish, the celebrated Palestinian poet, made a protracted stopover at the hotel and could often be seen talking with friends about politics and literature in the lobby or on the terrace. Nowadays, the hotel's tea lounge, Day and Night, has become a meeting place for young couples on dates. The hotel will be completely renovated within one or two years.

On the south side of the Semiramis is Shepheard's Hotel. The old building, on Gumhoureya Street, was burned and gutted in 1952 when a mob attacked it. Shepheard's was rebuilt on the banks of the Nile. Traditionally one of Cairo's top social spots, the hotel comes alive at night when elderly gentlemen, their heads swathed in red tarboosh, and elegant women, their glittering gold ornaments jingling, meet in the lobby to enjoy a few hours of refined and desultory conversation, sometimes speaking only in English or French.

South of Shepheard's Hotel is the area where the foreign embassies are clustered. Known as the "Garden City," the area is near Roda Island where the eye-catching Hotel Meridien is located. In French "*meridien*" means "afternoon nap," and in the dry climate of Cairo, where one tires easily, it seems to beckon one to stop in and take a short rest while gazing at the calm waters of the Nile. This is sound advice in Egypt where the newcomer and the unwary may be tempted not to waste time napping when the afternoon hours could be used for sightseeing. Wandering about at three o'clock, the hottest time of the afternoon, is ill-advised, and anyone doing so is inviting a sunstroke.

In the eighth century, the Nilometer was built on the south side of Roda Island to measure the rise and fall of the volume of water in the river. During the summer two boats, which have been converted into floating restaurants, are moored in front of the Hilton Hotel. The larger is known as Osiris, and the smaller as Isis, after the god and goddess in Egyptian mythology. Ancient Egyptians believed that Osiris was slaughtered and his body scattered after being hacked to pieces. Isis, his wife, searched out the pieces one by one and buried them together at one place. Osiris is the god of the underworld, and Isis the goddess who protects the tombs. During the winter both boat-restaurants are floated to Aswan where they are docked for the season.

A stroll along the banks of the Nile inevitably includes small children, with outstretched hands, demanding, "Backsheesh." Some foreigners are apt to show their displeasure, but Egyptians always give something, no matter how little. I suppose this is the manifestation of the principle "From those who have to those who have not."

Sometimes a taxi driver will turn to a passenger and say "I've no change," and simply pocket the difference in the fare as backsheesh. Some might conclude that the drivers are misusing their religion—except that it works both ways. I have often found myself a few coins short of the exact fare, and most times the driver has let me off with a discount, a smile, a shake of the head and a whispered "*Maareish.*" There is this feeling that everybody occasionally has hard times, so it is best to approach life with a liberal dose of both give and take.

Stepping into Liberation Square at the back of the Hilton Hotel, one finds the Egyptian Museum right in front. A magnificent collection of artifacts are laid out rather haphazardly, and if a specialist devoted his whole life to browsing through the museum, he would never see everything there is to see. Some years ago when a number of the more precious items were being evaluated for insurance purposes, their value was estimated at around five billion Egyptian pounds (U.S. $13 billion).

The museum is cramped, some of the windows are broken, and occasionally birds fly into the exhibition hall. Only the exhibits in the Tutankhamen Collection have been well arranged, and there are plans for building a separate museum which will be entirely devoted to this collection. If it is built, "Old King Tut's" burial accouterments will be displayed in a museum located beside the Great Pyramids at Giza.

I must have visited the museum more than fifty times but one of the few things that always disappointed me was the fact that the Rosetta Stone displayed there is an imitation. The actual stone is housed in the British Museum in London. The Rosetta Stone was found in 1799 by Napoleon's invading armies. It contained identical inscriptions in ancient Egyptian hieroglyphics, demotic characters and ancient Greek. By comparing the three languages, the learned French Egyptologist Jean Francois Champollion in 1822 succeeded in deciphering the inscription. The deciphered hieroglyphs were the key that opened the gate to understanding ancient Egyptian civilization. Since I could not see the actual stone in Egypt, I tried to see it during a brief visit to London but could not even see it there because the stone was then on loan for an exhibition in Paris! The British Museum was, however, selling exact plaster replicas of the stone for as little as U.S. $100, and those surpassed the poor copy on display in the museum in Cairo.

The Rosetta Stone is not the only treasure that the Egyptians have lost. A native guide at the museum told me that much larger pieces such as famous obelisks and relics from the age of the Pharaohs had also been taken abroad, because, as he said, clenching his fists, "It is regrettable that in the past so many of our leaders were fools."

Most people think that the Red Sea and the Mediterranean

were linked for the first time by the opening of the Suez Canal, but there was a smaller canal already in existence at the time the Suez was opened, and through the ages there have been a number of canals connecting the Red Sea and the Nile. The earliest record of a water link between the two waters dates to the reign of Darius I who lived from B.C. 521 to 486. The Darius Stele exhibited in Gallery Thirty-Five in the east wing of the ground floor of the museum carries an inscription describing the celebrations marking the opening of a canal.

Just a short walk from where the ten roads meet in Liberation Square is the Kasr El Nil Theatre. Here Umm Kalthoum, the famous Egyptian singer, who was loved not only by her own people but by Arabs everywhere, occasionally gave recitals. She died in February, 1975, at the age of seventy-seven, but the songs she made famous—songs showing her love for the Arabs—are still played daily on the radio all over the Arab world, and her records are still selling. *Y Habibi—Oh! My Love*—which she was singing right up until her death, was her theme song. I can remember the sultry tones of her voice even now.

Mrs. Kalthoum had a most extraordinary voice. Whereas the ordinary singer can hold a single note for a maximum of forty seconds, she could hold a note for more than a minute and a half. Because the chorus was repeated, she could make one tune last for over two hours. Someone even did a doctoral thesis for the University of Cairo titled "An Analysis of the Voice of Umm Kalthoum." According to his thesis, her voice vibrated 14,000 times per second, three times that of the average person.

Mrs. Kalthoum's private villa was situated on the west bank of Zamalek, quite near my own apartment. During my strolls, I often saw her sitting on the verandah of her rose-colored villa overlooking the Nile drinking tea with her family.

On the eastern edge of the 26 of July Street are the Ezbekieh

Gardens, which were bound on one side by the Opera House. Built in 1869 to commemorate the opening of the Suez Canal, Verdi composed *Aida* to mark the construction of the Opera House. He was unable to finish *Aida* in time for the opening, so it was celebrated instead with a performance of the composer's *Rigoletto*. The Opera House had to wait three more years before its commemorative work was finally performed there.

The Opera House and all of its historical records were completely destroyed by fire one morning in 1971. No opera house has been built to take its place.

The fire was said to have been caused by a short circuit, but there has been some speculation as to why the fire was not discovered immediately and why it got out of control when there was a fire station so nearby. One of my journalist friends suggested it might have been because it was the time of Ramadan.

During the feast of Ramadan, the "morning meal" is traditionally eaten after sundown. The "main meal" of the day will be eaten in the middle of the night, and the "evening meal" just before sunrise. No food may be consumed after sunrise. Therefore everyone is awake all night, and with no food to look forward to during the day, they enjoy a hearty meal just before dawn. Like people everywhere, they follow a big meal by a long nap. When the Opera House fire broke out, the security guard was asleep, and by the time a passerby noticed the fire, it was already out of control.

At Ramadan, everyone is hungriest just before sunset. Anyone arriving at Cairo Airport at this particular time will find the immigration counter closed, and a long line of incoming passengers forming. The officer on duty will have decided that it would be all right to leave the immigration counter for a bit in order to eat his evening meal!

Nonbelievers caught in these religious circumstances are likely to be irritable and less than understanding. But I know that if I told an Egyptian that in Japan we cremate the body after death, they would be shocked that anyone could do such a cruel thing. It is only natural that we should be unable to grasp completely the different traditions of other religions. However, I feel the problems of understanding are rooted in differences that encompass more than religion alone. I think those differences evolve from the way an individual evaluates or views things. It may be that Buddhism and Mohammedanism do not overlap as much as Mohammedanism and Christianity, but there appears to be greater dissimilarities between Japan and the Middle Eastern nations, than, for example between Middle Eastern nations and those of Europe or the Americas.

On Adly Road, going west from Opera Square is a tea shop called "Groppy" which serves the most delicious ice cream and sherbet I have ever tasted. King Hussein of Jordan is supposed to be extremely fond of it and reportedly he orders from the shop whenever he comes to Cairo. There is also a restaurant and grocery store with the same name on Talaat Harb Square, famous for its dried fish roe which is sold as a souvenir to foreign tourists.

The famous Continental-Savoy Hotel stands in front of Opera House Square. An old hotel, it became the favorite of archaeologists engaged in the 1922 excavation of the tomb of Tutankhamen. From the balcony of the hotel, the view includes the luxuriant growth of the trees in the Ezbekieh Gardens, Mt. Mokkatthuam, the twin minarets and the beautiful soft green dome of the Mohammed Ali Mosque in the distance.

The site where the mosque now stands was once occupied by the Citadel of Saladin, the fort of the brave Saracen warrior who broke up the armies of the Crusaders. The area northeast and southwest of the citadel is a living historical stage crowded with exquisite mosques and the Khan-el-Khalili Bazaar, the City of the Dead, and Old Cairo.

Son et Lumière performances given every evening at the Citadel of Saladin relive the past. In A.D. 641, General Amr of the advancing Islamic army made his camp on the east bank of the Nile at the spot known as "Al Fustat" (The Tent) which later became the site of the city of Cairo. Amr Mosque, built by General Amr is the oldest mosque in Cairo. It still exists today at Al Fustat, as do the remains of part of the walls of the old citadel. At its height, this was a flourishing capital, second only to Bagdhad. With the discovery of a number of relics of Chinese pottery in the vicinity in recent years, there is growing interest in the theory that the Silk Road, which linked the Middle and Near East with China, may have come as far as Al Fustat.

The town moved every hundred years or so, mirroring the changes in the dynasties. In A.D. 751, with a military dynasty, it was called Aska. In A.D. 870, this was superceded by Qataiya, which in turn was followed in 969 by a move towards the north with the advent of a new dynasty.

During the Fatamite Dynasty (904–1171), the rulers ordered a new capital to be built. As the architects worked through the night to design the new capital, the light of the planet Mars, which they knew, inspired them. The name of this planet, *Kahira*, was given to the new capital. *Kahira*, which also has the meaning of "victory," was rendered in English as Cairo—the name of the present city.

This is the story that is retold nightly on the stage of the old citadel. In the nineteenth century, Mohammed Ali, who had been dispatched by the Turks, lured about 500 Mameluke soldiers into the citadel, and then, suddenly closing the gates, killed them all—just one tale in the bloody history of the citadel. War-

riors killed in the battle were buried in the cemetry at the foot
of Mt. Mokkatthuam.

Old Cairo is pervaded by smells of earth and sweat. On entering this part of the town, one is bombarded by dust, noise and
perfume. Foul-smelling piles of rotting fruit and vegetable scraps
are thrown daily into the streets. Energetic children splash enthusiastically in the muddy puddles that spot the street. The area
pulsates positively with life. But it also has several taxidermists'
shops, and it is a rather weird feeling watching a taxidermist pre-
pare a stuffed animal or bird and wondering whether he would
be able to undertake the mummification of a human being.

No tourist leaves Cairo without visiting the 600-year-old
Khan-el-Khalili Bazaar. Its tiny, winding streets glitter with gold,
silver and copper jewelry. They overflow with leather crafts,
accessories and antiques of every kind. The air is heavy with an
exotic mixture of the smell of roast lamb, the street cries of fresh
water vendors and the wafting fragrance of incense of every
imaginable kind. For some, the scents can be a bit heady and are
likely to cause a sneeze or two. The bazaar features shops selling
dubious aphrodisiacs. According to one proprietor, the main
component comes from some part of a whale and can be taken in
coffee. He needs no encouragement to show off bundles of letters, reputedly to have been sent in appreciation from "satisfied
customers" around the world. With a grin, he will say, "Of
course, I can guarantee absolutely satisfactory results."

Goods in the bazaar are not priced, and it is not necessary to
pay the asking price for anything. One is expected to haggle over
prices until a price is reached that is acceptable both to the customer and the merchant.

Hefty Egyptian women will bargain in loud voices, fingering

the merchandise while haggling over the price. Watching them, it almost seems as if the statue of Nofret has escaped from her exhibit in the museum, as they have luxurious hair and enormous eyes outlined with thick lines of kohl. Even when a really beautiful women is shopping, she will cast off her inhibitions to haggle over prices in rough tones, as if the family were parting with its last pound. She usually stalks out of the shop, indignantly refusing to buy anything. The proprietor rushes after her and makes another offer, and there in the street she beats him down to the price she is prepared to pay.

The really difficult thing to buy is antiques. How can anyone really tell if something priced at a hundred or a thousand dollars is the genuine article? A real expert will hold an object up to the light, sniff at it and finger it to test the feel with their bare hands. Some shops issue guarantees that the article is genuine, but then, who can say if the guarantee is authentic?

Tourists are regularly approached by Egyptians who promise them a good price for their U.S. dollars on the black market. Unwary tourists who have been taken in have sometimes found themselves being informed that the tout is in fact a police officer and that they are under arrest.

In the bazaar, fakes are mixed up with the genuine article in more ways than one. But after being duped a number of times, one gradually develops a discerning eye for the genuine article. When it comes to the value of experience, the Khan-el-Khalili Bazaar is the lesson of life in miniature.

Close to the bazaar is the Azhar Mosque and University. Azhar University is the pinnacle of learning for Islamic studies. Both the mosque and the university are worth visiting. Islamic temples crowd the area, and some like the Sultan Hassan Mosque and the Ibn Touloun Mosque represent the peak of Saracenic culture. The architecture of these mosques is supposed to have had a profound influence on modern Western culture.

In the eastern suburbs of the city there stretches the so-called City of the Dead. Off-white houses are scattered haphazardly along the road, but apart from some used as the retreats of vagabonds and thieves, nothing comes here except wild dogs. The buildings house only the remains of the dead. Once a year the relatives and families of the dead gather together and hold a feast. Most of the owners of the houses are wealthy, but there are some plaques that commemorate the soldiers killed in the Palestinian War. The fact that burial customs differ so widely in the Middle East from country to country seems strange to me. In Saudi Arabia, the body of the assassinated King Faisal is buried in a plot of vacant land, and the spot is marked only by a rude stone.

As its name implies, the City of the Dead embraces the concept that the environment should provide the dead with everything they need for "life," which shows that the attachment to the concept of a world after death, so obvious in the age of the Pharaohs, is still a part of Egyptian thinking.

42   CAIRO

1–4. An Egyptian boat with a typical flower-shaped prow passes in front of the 180-meter Cairo Tower, completed in 1957, and the Al Burg Hotel (*preceding page*). The aerial view at *right* shows Gezira Island, the nucleus of Cairo, girdled by blue bands of the Nile. A holiday in Cairo means sailing on the Nile (*below*) and admiring the beauty of the river in the quiet glow before sunrise (*opposite*).

5. Shown *below* is a plant closely associated with Egyptian history—the papyrus. 6. The Nilometer on the southern tip of Roda Island (*right*) was constructed by the ancient Egyptians, and only replaced in the last 15 years by the Aswan High Dam. 7. Tahrir Square is the traffic, business and cultural center of Cairo. 8. A rare cloudy day envelops the Mohammed Ali Mosque in mist (*opposite*).

9–12. A city of one thousand minarets, Cairo has an Islamic heritage that is given expression in practically every quarter. *Right*: An Islamic calendar indicating the religious events of the year is found in most households. *Below* and *opposite*: The panorama of central Cairo as seen from Ibn Touloun Mosque—minarets soar heavenward amid clusters of modern buildings. *Overleaf*: Mosques seen from the City of the Dead.

13–16. Arabesques on the ceilings (*below*) contribute to the fame of the tomb-mosque of Sultan Qaitbei built by the Sultan in A.D. 476. The Sultan Hassan Mosque (*right*) was constructed by its namesake in A.D. 764. The El Azhar Mosque (*bottom*) was built when the Fatamite Dynasty transferred its capital to Cairo. The domes of the Mohammed Ali Mosque (*opposite*) echo the style of mosques in Istanbul.

17–19. Women worship in the Ibn Touloun Mosque (*below*). Even today men and women pray in different areas of the mosque. *Right*: The wall surrounding the Ibn Touloun Mosque casts jagged shadows across the courtyard. *Overleaf:* A devout Muslim prays five times a day—at dawn, midday, afternoon, sunset and before retiring. Prayers at midday on Fridays are held in mosques.

20. Coffee houses abound in Cairo and the grounds left in one's cup reveal one's fate. 21. Chefs at the Nile Hilton Hotel create the gourmet dishes for which the hotel's fashionable restaurants are known. 22. The Nasser Mausoleum is covered with flowers on September 28, the anniversary of President Gamal Nasser's death. 23. A Cairo policeman surveys the traffic.

SUNERLAND

24–30. The Ataba and Khan-el-Khalili bazaars are bright with color and fragrant with spices. *Below* and *right*: A vendor of hard, salty bread and a woman peddling fowl. *Bottom*: During Ramadan, the open-air markets are bustling till late at night. *Opposite, from upper left*: smoker placidly drawing on a water pipe, woman in *galabia*, vendor of pigeons, haberdasher waiting for customers.

31. *Preceding page*: Unglazed jugs called *qulla* in a shop in old Cairo create this scene that might remind one of the tale of Ali Baba. 32–34. The city at work— woman weaving a carpet, butcher cutting a side of beef, and vendors at a vegetable market near Bab el Nasr. 35. *Opposite*: This tannery turns out fine leather products.

36–39. The belly dancer is an omnipresent feature of Cairo's night life. A sensual dance common to the Arab world, it is accompanied by flutes, stringed instruments and the beat of drums. 40. *Bottom*: The Cairo skyline from Garden City.

41–43. Egypt's political capital is also the national center of education. Shown here are students at the College of Applied Arts, drawing and sculpting.

44. *Opposite*: Forty-thousand students, many of them from Third World nations, are enrolled at Cairo University. The university is comprised of twenty-one faculties and research institutes, of which fifteen are located in downtown Cairo.

45–49. Jewelry, masks and statuary are some of the treasures in the Egyptian Museum. *Below* and *right*|: A gold pendant and a Fifth Dynasty statue of Ka-Aper. The 110-centimeter wood figure was excavated in 1866 at Saqqarah. *Below, left* and *right*: Ra-Hotep and his wife of legendary beauty, Nofret, Fourth Dynasty from Meidum. *Opposite*: The golden funerary mask of King Tutankhamen, Eighteenth Dynasty.

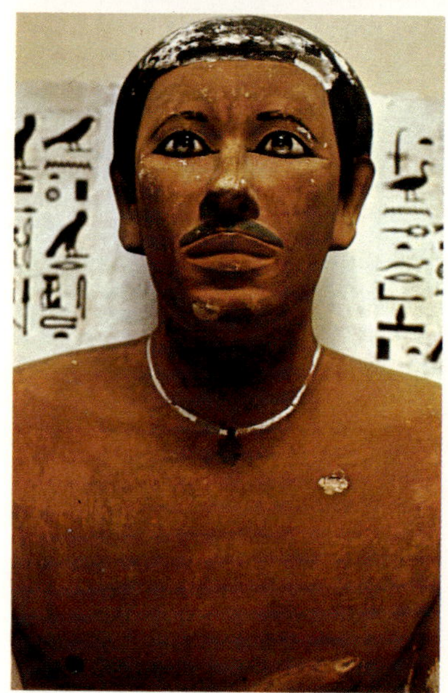

50–52. The Islamic Art Museum has a
fine collection *Below*: Intricate patterns
on tile. *Right*: Luster-ware plate with
a design of a woman playing an oud.
Bottom: The entrance to a mosque.
53–55. A fresco in the Coptic Museum
(*opposite, upper left*) portrays Adam and
Eve, and the picture on a curtain (*upper
right*) is floutist. *Opposite, bottom*: Saqqarah Hall. 56. *Overleaf*: The Mukhtar
Museum has modern art exhibits.

The Great Pyramids

and Other Monuments

The Greek historian Herodotus said of the Nile, "It is the gods' gift to Egypt"; and indeed, without the Nile, Egypt could not exist. The great river is the life force of the country, and the development of Egypt has depended on the Nile for the thin strip of fertile land that runs along its banks through the center of the country. Before it splays into the Delta, the Nile is a narrow blue strip, edged with green, which divides the vast wastes of the desert into the Western and Eastern deserts. One theory advanced as an explanation of the highly developed state of geometry in Ancient Egypt is the symmetry of line afforded by the contrast of the river bordered on either side by the desolate sands of the desert, stretching in both directions as far as the eye can see. Whether Egypt's geometry is connected with its geography is difficult to say, but it is interesting to note that the present-day City of the Dead on the east bank of the river in Cairo is balanced on the western bank at nearby Giza by the Great Pyramids, which we can call the "ancient City of the Dead," dating back to the age of the Pharaohs.

The road from Cairo to Giza runs directly south from the Sheraton Hotel. The sights of that road include the dome roof of Cairo University and the luxuriant foliage of the trees flourishing in the Cairo Zoo. One of the zoo's more unusal inmates is a rare bird called a "shoe-bill" because its great flattened bill looks like a shoe. The Egyptians call it, rather endearingly, "Papa of a Shoe." Although the animal really is rather grotesque, it is quite oblivious to its appearance and happily struts about its home in the zoo.

Farther south, the street crosses Ahram Road, which leads to the Great Pyramids. "*Ahram*," the Arabic word for "pyramid," is also the name of the country's leading daily newspaper, which bears as its logo three red pyramids on its front page.

On both sides of Ahram Road, vendors sell sweet corn, watermelons and *qulla* (earthenware urns). *Qulla* are natural water coolers and are the Egyptians' way of ensuring a supply of delicious cool water even in this hot climate. Because the urns are made of earthenware and are unglazed, the water inside slowly seeps out to the surface and rapidly evaporates. The action of seepage and evaporation keeps the water in the pot cool, so that even if the urn is left in the sun, the water inside will always be refreshing.

At the outskirts of the city, modern buildings no longer dominate the scenery, which has acquired a rural expression. The semi-pastoral scene is blighted, however, by a conglomeration of small shacks. These are the nightclubs of which the most famous is L'Auberge des Pyramides. At night the neon signs sparkle, giving the area an exotic appearance. So it is only in the daytime that the place seems shabby and desolate, a little like a mature woman who looks drab without her make-up.

Soon the familiar shapes of the Great Pyramids rise into view. I had a rather strange sensation as my car approached them. It was as if the Pyramids were receding into the distance, giving me the impression that it would take ages to reach them. In fact, they are no more than a fifteen-to-twenty-minute drive from central Cairo. But before the days of the automobile, it took three hours by donkey to reach them, which probably heightened a traveler's anticipation.

As one moves out to meet the desert, the town and villages fostered by the waters of the Nile abruptly come to an end. The true border between the settlements along the Nile and the desert proper are the Pyramids. Behind them stretches the vast desert, a seemingly endless expanse of sand. In fact, it covers the whole western part of Egypt, eventually merging with the sands of the Libyan Desert.

The first time I visited the Pyramids was towards evening. As I stood gazing up at these enormous monuments—at the same time trying to get rid of someone pestering me to ride a camel—other sightseers were gradually making their way back to their hotels. Even as I watched, the sun, a great red ball, was setting rapidly somewhere beyond the Libyan Desert, coloring the Pyramids with a variety of hues. The shadows cast by the Pyramids are unbelievably large; their huge forms rob whole areas of the late afternoon light, dyeing them an impenetrable black. The monoliths are stark and beautiful in their geometric simplicity and need no embellishments from me.

As I stood entranced by their form, a cool breeze began to blow and from somewhere there came the resonant voice of the muezzin calling the faithful to prayer. I felt that if the sound of silence exists, this is what it would be like; it was as if I were lost in eternity. Mundane matters—my job and personal problems—suddenly seemed to be of no importance. The sight of these Pyramids, urged me to think more profound thoughts, to contemplate the significance of man, life, death, history and of time itself. Looking at these massive crumbling stone monuments, my sense of time became hazy and dulled by distance. The realization of the transience of human existence and man's impotence seemed to be born in me in a single moment. Albert Camus once wrote about the desert: "It is a place where no one can live, but there is no doubt that some will consider a way of doing so."

I cannot say why, but I felt a peace of mind difficult to describe. I seemed to comprehend how the religion of Islam could be born out of the harshness that is the desert. The people of the desert cleanse their hands by rubbing them with sand, and it seemed to me that sand can also purify the spirit. My irritation of a few minutes earlier now seemed foolish. It did not matter that, unbidden, a guide had actually got into my car, or that, after having taken a photograph of some camels in the distance, I was asked to pay for the privilege. So without a motion of protest and without speaking a word, I placed a little backsheesh into the outstretched hand of the small boy who approached me. "*Shukran*"— hand clenched over his chest in the traditional Arab greeting—the boy expressed his thanks, and I found it a very beautiful gesture. I marvelled at myself. The Pyramids and the desert were having a profound effect on my state of mind.

When he was alive, Nasser maintained a villa in the vicinity of the Pyramids, and now, so does President Sadat. Exhausted by politics, he comes here to revive himself, to gaze out over the desert and the Pyramids, to become lost in his thoughts.

When I entered the Great Pyramid of Khufu, or Cheops, a surprisingly commonplace odor greeted me. I was taken to the Pyramids for the first time by an Egyptian, a journalist friend. Before setting out he had entertained me handsomely to some typical Arab cuisine and I had made a hearty meal of *sheshkebabs*, chunks of lamb and vegetables roasted on skewers, washed down with generous drafts of *arak*, a strong local drink, off-white in color, drunk slightly diluted with water. We had eaten the meal in the accepted way, with our fingers, and the pungent smell of the lamb still clung to us. Wandering up and down the stairs inside the Pyramid our hands rubbed continuously against the handrails, as those of countless Egyptians had done before us. In doing so, we were all transferring the odor of our meal into the raïls, with the result that Cairo's omnipresent smell of mutton is even part of the still air in the innermost chambers of the centuries-old Pyramids at Giza.

Most visitors to the Pyramids want to climb to the very top of these mountainous monuments. There is an ancient inscription which refers to them as the "slopes to heaven," perhaps reflecting the desire of the Pharaohs, which was to reach the sun after death. I, for one, would have liked to have had the experience of standing on the very summit of a Pyramid, but scaling one of their steep slopes is considered dangerous and it is forbidden to climb to the top.

This was not always the case, and at one time there was an official guide dubbed the "Acrobat King of the Pyramids." A slightly built man, Nefnawi Faid is now around fifty years old, but he is still famous for holding the record for the shortest time in scaling the Great Pyramid of Cheops—an amazing five minutes and thirty seconds to the top and back again. Nefnawi Faid first climbed the Pyramid when he was twenty-six. His performance came to be famous and his scaling of it became the regular conclusion to a visit to Cheops's tomb. Born in the nearby village of Mena, the Pyramids were his life. Heads of state and senior government officials on state visits have stood amid the crowds and shouted encouragement to the little man. A list of his excited cheerers would read like an international Who's Who— Nasser, Nehru, Sukarno, Chou En-Lai and Aneurin Bevan. When Khrushchev saw the performance he presented him with a gold watch. Yugoslavia's Tito, on witnessing it, gave him a gold cigarette case. King Faisal, a monarch rarely moved by anything, watched the performance with a look of disbelief on his face, and when Faid reached the ground he is said to have surprised him with 1,000 Egyptian pounds (approximately U.S. $2,500) on the spot. In his climb to the top of the Pyramid, Faid faced danger daily and never knew whether he would see another tomorrow. And so the story goes that when Faid received the generous present from King Faisal, he promptly announced that he would be taking a holiday and go drinking with his friends until all the money was gone!

Apparently, the secret of climbing a pyramid is not to do it in a straight line, but to zigzag up a side. Balance is extremely important, and it is vital to concentrate every second. Whatever happens, one must not be distracted from the climb.

When he married and settled down to become a family man in 1973, Faid began to think that it was time to give up the dangerous climb. The government at that time issued an order prohibiting the climbing of pyramids. As a result, Nixon, and later Kissinger, on their visits to Egypt were denied the opportunity of witnessing Faid's skill and speed. Glancing from his gold watch to the top of the Pyramids, Faid is not above musing about the "good old days."

The reason for the government order prohibiting the scaling of pyramids is twofold. Not only is it considered a dangerous risk, but it is also thought that if done too frequently the pyramids' sides will gradually be worn away. Originally constructed from over 2,500,000 square stones, each weighing two and a half tons, the Pyramids have been the victims of erosion and thievery. Now no more than 2,300,000 stones remain. There is a well-known story that Napoleon, on reaching the Pyramids with his armies, shouted to his men, "Four thousand years of history is looking down on you. These stones would be sufficient to build a wall ten feet high and a foot wide to enclose France completely."

At the time it was built, Cheops Pyramids was 480 feet high. But it has been eroded to 450 feet. The top does not come to a point, but is square and flat. Originally it was only 10 feet square, but the effects of erosion have taken their toll and the top now measures 33 feet square.

What sort of man was Cheops to have had at his disposal the organization and technical skill required to construct these great masses of stone? Some say he was a powerful and cruel tyrant who sought only personal glory. But perhaps the masses who actually built the Pyramids were content with the belief that participation in the construction of the monument for the king's "life after death" would secure them a small corner in that same world.

Southwest of Cheops' Pyramid stand the other two Great Pyramids—of Chephen and Mycerinus. The Great Sphinx is located a little to the east of them. The Sphinx, its face the face of the ruler Chephen and its body that of a lion, gazes over the desert typifying everything that was Egypt in the days of the Pharaohs.

The Sphinx is the main actor in the nightly *Son et Lumière* performance at the Great Pyramids. Each evening the drama of thousands of years of history is reenacted with the aid of multicolored lights, accompanied by stately music and balanced, poetic narration. Although I have seen *Son et Lumière* performances at the Red Fort in India and at Persepolis in Iran, I found the performance at the Sphinx the most compelling, possibly because of the ability of the Sphinx to conjure up thousands of years of history right before one's eyes.

With the pauses in narration, the silence is profoundly eloquent. Then the narration picks the story up again:

"With each new dawn I see the Sun-god rise on the bank of the Nile. His first ray is for my face. And for five thousand years I have seen all the suns men can remember come up in the sky. . .

"I saw Anthony and Cleopatra pass. Alexander, Caesar and

Napoleon passed at my feet. I saw the ambitious dreams of con-
querors whirling like dead leaves. . . .

"Centuries passed over my forehead yet those great soldiers
raised no more than dust. . . .

"In the course of time, only human achievements crumble and
fall but the spirit which conceived these monuments cannot
perish."

The Sphinx falls silent. The lights go out. He has suggested the
truth about man's impotence and the transience of all things.

The impression created by the Pyramids is constantly chang-
ing, differing with the time of day. Similarly, the view from the
Pyramids is different from every direction. If a sightseer goes to
Giza, he can stay at the Hotel Mena House, located just below
the Pyramids. It was here, in 1943, that Roosevelt, Churchill and
Chiang Kai-shek met and issued the Cairo Declaration, the docu-
ment containing the conditions for ending World War II. Guests
can gaze at the Pyramids bathed in moonlight or under the harsh
glare of the midday sun and breathe the pure air of the desert.
People relaxing on the terrace with a glass of beer or a cup of
tea, occasionally raise their heads in the direction of the Pyramids. Some guests set out on horseback from the front of the
hotel—the novices with guides leading the horses, and the more
experienced taking the reins and galloping off in fine style, bring-
ing to mind thoughts of Lawrence of Arabia.

From the Hotel Mena House it takes an hour on horseback for
the round-trip excursion to Sahara City. "*Sahara*" means "desert,"
and as the name implies, the city lies right in the middle of the
desert. The city itself is really just a collection of tents which are
nightclubs. The nightclubs operate throughout the summer
season with their own belly dancers.

A few of the more adventurous tourists do their sightseeing
from the back of a camel. Staying on a camel's back, especially

with the disturbing undulating motion as the animal walks, can be hard work if the rider is inexperienced, so this should be carefully considered before attempting camel riding.

The turf of the golf course in front of the hotel is not the best because of the dry desert climate. Nevertheless, there is a rather expansive feeling about taking a swing in the direction of the Pyramids, as if one is somehow propelling a small white ball backward in time, through thousands of years to antiquity.

Many tourists erroneously think that the three Great Pyramids at Giza are the only ones in Egypt, but there are actually some sixty or more located a little further south. The most famous of these lesser-known monuments is the Step Pyramid of Saqqarah. The Step Pyramid was built around 2800 B.C. for King Zoser Neterikhet. The king had come from Nubia in the south and established the Memphis Dynasty which ruled the Sinai Peninsula and Nubia. He constructed a capital at Memphis on the west bank of the Nile, just east of the pyramid fields at Saqqarah. These pyramids were the burial places of the kings of Memphis, but at the city of Memphis is a small alabaster sphinx with the face of Rameses II and a mammoth statue of him lying full-length on the sand. Erosion has done its work on the part of the statue directly in contact with the sand so that it now crumbles away at a touch. A second statue of Rameses II was moved from Memphis in 1955 and placed in front of Cairo Central Station.

A sight that should not be missed at Saqqarah is the Serapeum, one of the subterranean tombs of the sacred Apis bulls. In the great alabaster slab containing their mummified remains, one can almost see the animals' blood flowing in the veins.

Today, Memphis is a scattering of low houses, their mud walls punctured with little holes to let the light in, and here and there daubed with Arabic graffitti painted in red or green. Looking at the place as it is now, it is difficult to realize that one of the greatest cities in the world once stood here. Though its power gradually waned, Memphis remained a powerful city for over three thousand years until its glory was usurped by the arrival in the seventh century of the Islamic armies and by the building of Al Fustat.

The traditional explanation of why the Citadel of Fustat was built on the east bank of the Nile has its roots in the Islamic religion. The invading armies chose their strategic point on the side of the river nearest to Mecca, the religious center of Islam, so that no water should flow between them and the Holy City.

The monument housing the tomb of King Zoser at Saqqarah is the oldest of all the pyramids. Though it has deteriorated into ruins there is nothing "dead" about it, rather it seems to exude a kind of vibrancy, and its strength matches the geometric beauty of the Great Pyramids at Giza.

Although the Great Pyramids at Giza are better known, the pyramids at Saqqarah are of more interest to people who are familiar with Egypt and its history. A number of the tombs and shrines of the nobility of Memphis in the vicinity of Saqqarah have been excavated and have offered a significant insight into life in ancient Egypt. The tomb of the high court official Ti in particular reveals a great deal of information about daily life through the drawings and paintings on the walls and pillars of the tomb. A wide variety of commonplace, everyday scenes are painted in the picture—farming scenes, men fishing, crocodiles, sports contests, tax collectors, religious festivals, chickens being cooked, maize being threshed, people tending geese, teachers and pupils in their classrooms, hospitals where operations are being performed. Every facet of life is depicted in the stiff, straight style peculiar to the ancient Egyptians. Still these drawings exhibit vigor, intense color and movement. Even the paint here looks as if it might have been applied recently.

Some of the scenes painted on the walls of the tomb are what the ancients believed in and hoped for after death. Because these people loved life, they believed that death was no barrier to life, which continued after death in a better, richer form. The splendor of this wonderfully vivid artistic technique is unknown in the modern world. A visit to the monuments and tombs of Saqqarah makes one wonder whether man has in fact progressed since the ascendancy of Memphis and the Pharaohs.

It was believed that after death the soul crossed the Nile by boat to begin life after death on the western bank of the river. Here the dead would enjoy everything they had enjoyed in life surrounded by beauty, fragrance and plenty. For this reason, the dead were mummified and placed in beautiful, exquisitely decorated caskets shaped to the body. Their tombs were filled with all the requisites of daily life from gold, silver and jewels to instruments to till the soil. The richness of the treasures in the tombs inevitably excited the avaricious, so through the ages the tombs were plundered and many valuable items were stolen. Theory has it that in later burials articles were instead represented by drawings and paintings of everyday scenes on the wall.

Even today, it is not too unusual for one to find, while walking in the sand, fragments of the past life, shards of a bygone age. When visiting these places, I would often walk with my eyes cast down, searching the sand around my feet. Although I never found anything of significance, I heard of someone who found what appeared to be part of a woman's necklace this way. It is likely that a number of these fragments were dropped as thieves made their getaway, carrying out their plunder under the cover of night. The restless, constant movement of the sands would soon bury from view the articles they dropped, and they remain undiscovered until that same movement of the sand reveals them once again. I found the image of these plunderers,

backs bent, heaving under the burden of their spoils, an extremely vivid and exciting one.

The thought of these plunderers and treasure-seekers always
calls to mind a story I heard of a little Japanese girl from Kyoto.
The girl became sick and died while still quite young, but all
through her short life she dreamed of visiting the Pyramids.
After her death, her father took part of her ashes to Egypt and
buried them in the sand beside the Pyramids. He put the small
items she used into her little grave and set up a small tomb stone,
a tiny, modern pyramid. Some years later, visitors to the site,
could find no trace of the grave or any of the little items buried
there.

With the passage of time, the Egyptians ceased to build mighty
pyramids, highly visible in the empty desert, inviting desecration
and plunder. Instead, they built underground tombs, and in the
Valley of the Kings of Luxor several hundred kilometers upstream
from Saqqarah, the tombs of the Pharaohs are buried deep in the
limestone hills on the western side of the Nile. Even here the
great majority of tombs have been plundered, but the tomb of
Tutankhamen was fortunately found intact in 1922. This was
one of the greatest archaeological finds of all time. Excavation of
the tomb is still going on today. Unfortunately, the finds have
not only been removed by the official excavators. Groups of
professional antique hunters masquerading as excavators are also
active. Not infrequently a customer in a Cairo antique shop will
be told, "This has recently been excavated. . . ."

Another of the significant remains to be found at Saqqarah are
the catacombs of the tomb of Apis, the Sacred Bull of Ptah. The
tomb was built to house the mummified remains of the great
bull Apis, believed to be the incarnation of Ptah, the god of
Memphis. The great, stuffy, gloomy underground passages of

the catacombs are made up of numerous burial chambers as well as massive black granite slabs. The slabs were used for animal worship and they give off a dull light which is more uncanny than awe-inspiring.

The man who designed the Step Pyramid at Saqqarah was Imhotep, an architect, historian, a man of letters, and a doctor. Much time and effort has been spent searching for his tomb because it is believed that it contains the key to understanding the civilization of ancient Egypt. An English Egyptologist, Walter Emery, devoted the last seven years of his life to searching for the great architect's tomb, but without success.

Asked if he had found anything, Emery softly replied, "If you carry on digging for ten years, you might, you just might, find one thing of significance in all that time." His search did not stop until his death. Not even the Seven-Day War in 1967 brought it to a halt. On March 7, 1971, while he was hunting for Imhotep's tomb, he had a heart attack. He was rushed to hospital in Cairo, where he died three days later.

Imhotep was said to have been very fond of the crested ibis, a bird native to Egypt, therefore it is likely that there would be a number of these painted in his tomb to accompany him into his life after death. With the discovery in 1970 of an urn containing the mummified remains of a number of ibis, Emery hoped that at last the tomb of Imhotep had been discovered. Soon after, Emery unearthed a strange box, small and rectangular in shape. Brushing away the sand, Emery opened it to it to find it contained a tiny statue of the God of Death, Anubis. A moment later, he keeled over, stricken by the heart attack which ended his life at the age of sixty-eight.

The circumstances of Emery's death were fully reported in the Egyptian newspapers. It became the latest death to be added to those blamed on the so-called Curse of the Pharaohs. There have been a number of mysterious deaths among the people who investigate the ancient ruins of Egypt, deaths for which there is no apparent logical explanation. Some are attributed to the Curse of the Pharaohs.

The first victim of the curse is considered to be Lord Carnarvon, an English nobleman who was a member of the party excavating the tomb of Tutankhamen. The tomb was discovered in 1922, and in the following year, Lord Carnarvon was stung on the cheek by a mosquito while at the site in the Valley of the Kings. The bite turned septic and resulted in his death by blood poisoning. The story goes that at the moment of his death the entire city of Cairo was plunged into darkness by a sudden power failure. The idea of a curse seems to have been actually generated by the English mystery writer Sir Arthur Conan Doyle who, writing of the incident, remarked, "His Lordship's death may possibly have been the result of elements laid down by the priests of Tutankhamen, to protect the Pharaoh's tomb."

Since the death of Lord Carnarvon, there have been about twenty people connected with the excavations whose deaths, in road accidents, by suicide or assassination, have been linked to the curse. Some people claim that at the entrance to the tomb of Tutankhamen there is a notice with the warning: "Anyone touching the tombs of the Pharaohs is likely to invite sudden death."

Of course, there are many who scoff at the idea of a curse. Leonard Cottrell, an English archeologist and commentator, temporarily ended the argument when he wrote that the three most important people connected with the excavation of the Tutankhamen's tomb, including Howard Carter, the man who actually discovered it, all survived to live completely normal lives. After a considerable lapse of time, however, the controversy flared up again with the recent death of Emery. It is possible that Egyptians simply enjoy events draped in the cloth of mystery. But today, with so many mysteries still unsolved by modern science, people may retain an incomprehensibly strong feeling of morbid curiosity about such things and a belief in the existence of a world of malevolent spirits. Supporting my theory is the popularity of books and movies dealing with the occult, particularly the demonic occult. For instance in the mid-1970's, movie-goers flocked to theaters to be scared by such films as *The Exorcist* and *The Omen*.

No less thrilling than the pyramid fields and hillside tombs, complete with the story of the curse of the Pharaohs, is the great labyrinth of Fayum. The Fayum is located to the west of the Nile, about one hundred kilometers south of Memphis. The labyrinth was a great palace built by King Amenemhat III, a ruler of the Twelfth Dynasty (2000—1785 B.C.). Visiting the Fayum in the fifth century B.C., Herodotus expressed his profound amazement at the wonder of the labyrinth: "I have seen the labyrinth with my own eyes, but its wonder defies description, not all the mansions and monuments in all of Greece, if gathered together, could compare in terms of magnitude, in labor and cost to the labyrinth of Fayum. It exceeds the Pyramids."

This labyrinth, as its name implies, is a vast complex of over 3,000 rooms stretching both above and below the ground, joined by a maze of passages, a veritable honeycomb. Yet the words of Herodotus tell only half the story, for apparently, he was only allowed to see the upper rooms.

The part of the labyrinth that was above ground has long since crumbled away to dust, but it is believed that the underground passages still exist somewhere under the lush green of this oasis. On June 3, 1974, it was announced that the tomb of a Pharaoh, estimated to have been built around 2000 B.C., had been discovered fifteen meters below the surface. The tomb contained numerous artifacts along with a magnificent stone sarcophagus inlaid with gold. Excavation was started at once, and it is possible that as progress is made part of the underground chambers of the labyrinth, which have so long remained hidden, will once again come to light.

Fayum, and the area immediately surrounding it, is below sea level and is the oasis closest to the Nile. It is on the west side. There, a number of flourishing agricultural settlements are gathered around Lake Qaroun, and the flavor of figs and chickens from this region is delicious. Fayum is also a prosperous rose-growing center, producing quantities of rose oil for domestic use and for export. When the roses are in bloom, they scent the entire region with their gentle perfume.

57. *Preceding page*: The Great Sphinx is said to have the face of King Chephen, the builder of the second of the three Great Pyramids. 58. Carriages bring tourists to the Pyramids. 59. The Great Pyramids of Giza were the tombs (*from left*) of Cheops, Chephen and Mycerinus. 60. *Opposite*: Visitors at the base of Cheops's Pyramid. 61. *Overleaf*: The grand stage of history—and of the *son et lumière* presentation.

62. "Ships of the desert" relaxing.

63. A desert scene near the Pyramid of Cheops.

64. *Opposite*: Camel drivers and their beasts wait in one spot near the Pyramids for adventurous tourists.

65. *Overleaf*: Relics from the Twenty-Sixth Dynasty have been unearthed at the excavation site in the Fayum which is pictured here.

66–69. *Right*: Detail of a relief on Mereruka's tomb, Sixth Dynasty. *Below left*: The text found at Unis's Pyramid at Saqqarah explains the religious beliefs of the ancient Egyptians. *Below right*: Ti's tomb wall, Fifth Dynasty. *Bottom*: The site excavated by Englishman Walter Emery. 70. *Opposite*: Balancing a *qulla* looks easy. 71. *Overleaf*: The Step Pyramid of King Zoser, is the oldest of the Egyptian pyramids.

72–74. Memphis, about 30 kilometers south of Cairo, was chosen by King Zoser as his capital. The city (*right*) is ringed by palms *Below*: The temple of the sacred bull Ptah was the center of religion before the ancient Egyptians turned to sun-worship. *Opposite*: One of the monumental statues of Rameses II. 75. *Overleaf*: The rhomboidal pyramid in Dahshur was constructed by King Sneferu, founder of the Fourth Dynasty.

Alexandria

Witness to Greatness

The invasion of Alexander the Great in the fourth century B.C., arrested the decline of the Pharaoh's power, providing a new leader for the government and even hope for the people. Alexander's subjugation of Egypt was swift. After a short pause at the foot of the Sphinx at Giza, his invading armies went on to conquer Memphis and then turned north, looking for an oasis. Reaching the coast he discovered Pharos Island in the Bay of Alexandria, or *Iskandariya*, as it is called as Arabic. He connected the island to the mainland, creating a wonderful harbor, and made it his stronghold, establishing the town of Alexandria here in 331 B.C.

The journey from Cairo to Alexandria takes three hours by train and five by road. As one heads for Alexandria by train, just to the right of Cairo Central Station is a building that is frequently overlooked but shouldn't be. This is the Railway Museum which contains fascinating information about the history of trains in Egypt. According to records in the museum, the first train ran from Alexandria to Cairo in 1852. Both the construction of the railroad and the production of the locomotives were handled by the Robert Stevenson Company, managed by the son of George Stevenson, inventor of the steam locomotive. Since the exhibits in the museum are not confined exclusively to the railroad, there is also much significant information on the history of transportation from the time of the Pharaohs, with interesting sketches depicting how thousands of laborers used logs and levers to move the great blocks of stone into place for the Great Pyramids.

The trains now running between Cairo and Alexandria were produced in Hungary. The reclining seats in the "Deluxe" coaches are very restful. Meals are served to the passengers at their seats on aluminum trays. These air-conditioned cars are so comfortable that they are even slightly more pleasant than those of Japan's "bullet train" which whizzes between Tokyo and Osaka.

But because these carriages are comfortable does not mean that the startling cannot happen when riding one. During a trip I was making on this line, a waiter suddenly appeared and prostrated himself at my feet. Naturally, I was astonished but convinced that he wished some great favor of me. I was mistaken, however, for without saying a word the man placed his forehead on the floor of the carriage and began praying, turned towards Mecca, while the train hurtled forward to Alexandria.

About fifteen miles out of Cairo, the train passes the Delta Barrage, the area known to Egyptians as Bath-el-Bakkarah—"The Cow's Stomach." Here the Nile branches into the Rosetta and Damietta rivers. Although Napoleon was the first to think of constructing a barrage here to control the amount of water flowing into the two rivers, the actual construction work was begun by Mohammed Ali in the nineteenth century. Irrigation has created a fertile area with arable land stretching as far as the eye can see, broken only by the tall sails of feluccas as they glide along the numerous irrigation canals which crisscross the Delta. To eyes only used to the dry, light brown color of the desert, the green and blue of this area is superbly refreshing. President Sadat was born and raised on a farm in the Delta. He describes himself as having the "quiet personality of the Egyptian farmer, having been brought up on a farm." He still maintains a country retreat in this area.

Although irrigation has transformed the Delta into a rich agricultural land, most of the farmhouses are still made of brick and mud. Delta homes are still not fully supplied with the amenities of running water and electricity so most of the water is drawn by hand and light is usually provided by oil lamps.

Families in rural areas tend to be large, and there is nothing extraordinary about a couple having six or seven children. Children are expected to work and are traditionally considered part of the labor force. The domestic animals—oxen, donkeys, goats, ducks and chickens—are treated as members of the family, so that a stay in an Egyptian farmhouse can result in being afflicted by fleas and all other manner of insects which plague domestic animals.

There are a number of cotton fields and vineyards in the Delta. Most of the grapes produced here are used for Egypt's flourishing wine industy. The domestic wines are often given such stirring names as "Ptolemy," one of the kings who ruled Alexandria when the city was at the height of its prosperity; "Aphrodite," the goddess of love; "Osiris," the god of the underworld; and "Omar Khayam," the poet. Farmers in the Delta rise early and ride their donkeys into the fields. Despite the complex irrigation system of the barrage, farming here has remained unchanged for centuries. The implements, hoes and ploughs, are rather small and water is drawn from the irrigation ditches by oxen or donkeys slowy treading round and round the same path. Water required for cooking is carried from wells in pitchers balanced on the women's heads so that the scene from a train window is almost like experiencing a huge time gap; the daily life of people during the time of the Pharaohs seems to have been revived.

Families in rural communities are not wealthy. Although the country people exhibit a quiet personality and have a strong sense of fatalism, an ever-increasing number of them are moving to the towns in search of a better life. The same phenomenon is occurring all over the world. And as in other countries, making it to the city does not guarantee a magic improvement in the standard of living. Too frequently the opposite is true. In one of his short novels, *The Scorpion*, Abd al-Rahman al-Sharkawi, a famous Egyptian writer and native of the Delta, describes the tragedy of people in the rural communities. His hero, a young man called Hassan, leaves the Delta where he was born to live in Cairo. But life is no better in the big city and Hassan returns to his village and finds work catching scorpions. He is paid one piasta for every scorpion he catches. A catch of ten or more means he can buy meat or a shirt. He is doing well, better than ever before, but one day he is stung on the foot by one of the creatures he hunts. . .

The climate of Alexandria is milder than that of Cairo. Facing the Mediterranean there is more rain, and in September, especially, the humidity is high. The fact that it is known as the city both of Alexander and of Cleopatra makes it a great attraction for tourists. Besides being intrigued by its history, tourist are lured there in summer by a number of fine beaches.

Historically, Alexandria's port has been even more important than Beirut, the main port of the Middle and Near East. Tense relations with Israel have driven consideration for everything else into the background so that Alexandria has been reduced to a less-than-lovely town. However, if peace returns and the city is cleaned up, Alexandria should turn into a better port and a charming city.

Alexandria was built on the site of the ancient village of Rhakotis. The actual spot lies a little south of the Central Station and is marked by Pompey's Column. Further south of Pompey's Column lies the monument known as Kom-el-Shogaba—"The Hill of Shards"—with its marvelous catacombs. These were built in three stories, the lowest of which now lies far below sea level. Nothing is known about the numerous burial chambers and tombs contained in the catacombs, not even if they are the graves of ordinary people or of nobility. The air of the burial chambers is always cool, even in the height of summer. Standing there in the subdued light, I could not help but contemplate the history of the country and the many unsolved mysteries that exist in Egypt.

The bulk of the construction of Alexandria was carried out by Ptolemy II Philadelphus, in the first half of the third century B.C. Ptolemy II was an extremely erudite monarch who undertook the building of both the great library of Alexandria and the lighthouse of Pharos. He made Alexandria a center of learning, inviting scholars from throughout the ancient world to help compile a history of Egypt. So much of Hellenic culture was infused into this part of the Mediterranean it was said that the only thing Alexandria lacked was the snow of the Greek mountains. All the great men of ancient times—the geometricans Euclid and Archimedes; Timochares, the astronomer; and the poets Callimachus and Appollonius—have strolled along the shores of the Mediterranean at Alexandria, enjoying the sea breezes that still cool the land.

Here in Alexandria in 30 B.C., Cleopatra placed the asp on her breast. Her suicide brought about the beginning of the decline of the great empire created by Alexander. Yet the traces of splendor that characterized Alexandria lingered on for centuries. When General Amr arrived in Alexandria at the head of the invading Islamic armies some six hundred years later, he sent an amazing description to Omar, caliph of Baghdad: "This is a truly breathtaking city. There are over 4,000 palaces, 4,000 public baths, 400 theaters and 1,200 parks." Little, however, is left in Alexandria to recall its days of greatness, although modern roads still follow the original pattern, running from the center in a north-south or east-west direction. This design was adopted in the original city to allow the northern breezes to blow through the town. Even today, the main trunk road of El Hurreya, follows the same route it did two thousand years ago when Cleopatra passed along it.

Pharos, the island which prompted Alexandria to establish his great city here and the landmark of this fine harbor, no longer exists. The only trace of it is in Ras-el-Tin—"The Headland of Figs"—which used to be joined to the northwest corner of the island, and which juts out between the western and eastern harbors. The western harbor was the main one and has a great breakwater running along it, but Pharos was located in the eastern harbor close to what is now Qaitbei Fort. The lighthouse on the Island of Pharos was one of the Seven Wonders of the Ancient World. Some 400 to 600 feet high, the Pharos lighthouse is said to have been constructed completely of white marble in steps comprising a set of four to eight flights of stairs in all. The lower staircases wound around a rectangular shaft and the upper ones around a circular one; all were enclosed by balustrades. An enormous bonfire was kept blazing at the very top of the tower day and night so that it looked like a "pillar of fire by night and a pillar of smoke by day." The lighthouse had over three hundred rooms with hundreds of windows facing every direction and was manned constantly by soldiers, so it was also extremely useful as a lookout point. An enormous mirror of translucent stone amplified the light of the bonfire on the top of the tower. The rays emitted from the lighthouse could be seen from three hundred miles at sea.

How and why did the lighthouse and the island disappear? Strangely enough, the answer appears only in legends. The lighthouse continued to fulfill an important military function after Egypt was conquered by the Islamic armies. As part of a carefully thought out plot, a rumor was circulated during the days of the Christian emperor, Constantinople, that a great hoard of treasure had been hidden beneath the lighthouse. In their lust for the treasure, the Arabs began to dismantle the lighthouse, only to realize halfway through the prodigious task that the rumor had been a ruse. They reconstructed the lighthouse but as they were replacing the mirror-stone, they dropped it from the top of the tower. It broke and was never replaced. The rest of the demolition was completed by nature. During the thirteenth century, the area was hit by a terrible earthquake and what remained of the lighthouse and the island disappeared into the sea. Nevertheless, the Great Lighthouse of Pharos is remembered today in a less tangible, but perhaps more enduring form in the words for "lighthouse" which are "pharos" in English, "phare" in French, and "faro" in Spanish and Italian. But this is the only testament indicating that the greatest lighthouse in the world stood here.

114   CAIRO

On the western point of the harbor, directly opposite Qaitbei, stands the Ras-el-Tin Palace, once the residence of King Farouk, the so-called Last Pharaoh of Egypt. When the revolution was initiated on July 23, 1952, King Farouk was staying in the Montazah Palace, about ten miles to the east of Ras-el-Tin. The drama of the revolution surrounding the king in Alexandria is an extremely human one, and one that I personally find fascinating.

Farouk was roused a little after one o'clock in the morning by a close and loyal friend, and the king immediately began the drive to Ras-el-Tin. Cannon on the Qaitbei Road were already aimed at the palace. The king made a request to both the British and American ambassadors for assistance to put down the coup d'état, but he received no reply. By this time, General Naguib and Colonel Sadat (now President Sadat) were ready to enter Alexandria. Opinion within the army itself was divided on the question of whether to capture the king and execute him. Nasser, who spearheaded the revolution and who remained behind in Cairo, feared that the execution of the king would trigger a blood bath. With the words "History will sentence him to death," Nasser sent him into exile and won the approval the people.

Early on the morning of the twenty-sixth, Naguib and Sadat sent a final communique to the king giving him until six o'clock that evening to abdicate and leave the country. His palace surrounded by troops, the king wept openly as he signed his name to the letter of abdication. Then, at 5:45 p.m., dressed in the white uniform of an admiral, he accepted the salute of the guards of honor for the last time. As the national anthem was played, the royal standard was lowered and given to Farouk. The royal yacht, the *Mahrousa*, which the royal family had previously used for pleasure, stood waiting. Slowly Farouk went on board, followed by the queen, the prince and the three princess (and two hundred pieces of luggage). General Naguib arrived as the yacht weighed anchor and he saluted his former king. Farouk returned his salute. Both remained silent for some time. At last Naguib spoke, "It was you who forced us to do what we have done." Farouk replied, "I know. You have done what I always intended to do myself." The meaning of Farouk's words remains an enigma to this day. Even Naguib could not understand them. The pleasure boat finally began to move and Farouk turned to offer advice to his former general: "Your job will be difficult. It isn't easy to govern Egypt."

As the ship went through the harbor, all the boats sounded their sirens in a final salute, and a frigate, the *Malik Farouk*, sounded a twenty-one-gun salute. It's hollow echo across the bay was the final concession from Naguib to the departing king. The abdication of Farouk brought to an end the dynasty of Mohammed Ali, which was initiated at the beginning of the nineteenth century.

Along Corniche Road, in the opposite direction of Farouk's final drive from El Montazah to Ras-el-Tin, are the crowded beaches of Stanley, San Stefano, Ramleh, Sidi Bishr and El Mandarah. Halfway along the road is an area called Cleopatra, which is where this famous queen had a palace and a temple. It is now a yachting and fishing club. Most Westerners think of the name Cleopatra as being synonymous with a beautiful woman. In Egypt today, "Cleopatra" is the name of a well-known, locally produced cigarette. Apparently the Egyptians themselves think of Nefertiti as the epitome of beauty. She was the wife of Pharaoh Akhenaton and was certainly a strikingly beautiful woman. Souvenir shops abound with plates and trays carrying her likeness and ornaments made in the shape of her silhouette. The original bust of Nefertiti was excavated at Tell-el-Amarna in central Egypt and is now one of the prized exhibits of the Dahlem Museum in West Berlin.

In both New York and London are obelisks known as Cleopatra's Needle. In fact these monuments have nothing to do with Cleopatra. They were originally set up at Heliopolis, near present-day Cairo Airport, as monuments to victorious battles during the era of Thothmes III (1504–1450 B.C.). Following the death of Cleopatra, the Romans transferred the obelisks to Alexandria to enhance the beauty of the city, and it was then that each acquired the name Cleopatra's Needles. The story of Cleopatra, her beauty and majesty, was well known outside Egypt, and thinking these obelisks had some fundamental connection with the queen, they were carried off by American and British expeditions to Egypt in the nineteenth century and set up in New York and London respectively.

The Montazah Palace, formerly the residence of Farouk, is surrounded by a large garden, with a number of other buildings standing nearby. The palace itself has been converted into a museum, and one of the buildings in the grounds is now a casino. The walls of the galleries in the three-story palace are hung with pictures, some depicting love scenes from the Middle Ages.

Twelve miles east of the Montazah Palace lies the El Mamura coast, where Sadat has his country retreat. I was fortunate on one occasion to interview the president's wife, Jehan, there. My real objective was an interview with the president himself, and I had hoped that I could somehow persuade Madame Sadat to intercede with him on my behalf. It was by appealing to Madame Dewi, the wife of Sukarno, that I managed to get an interview with him in Jakarta in 1965, and I was hoping to be as fortunate in securing an interview with the president of Egypt.

My interview with Madame Jehan Sadat took place over tea at a table on the beach. I noticed from the marks on the teacups and napkins that the Sadats were using the Palestine Hotel, which overlooks the sea at El Montazah, to do their catering. I found it very difficult to raise the subject of an interview with the president, and only managed to hint at my real intention at the very end of the interview by saying, "I hope most sincerely that the next time we meet, you will be accompanied by your husband the president." But Madame Sadat merely acknowledged this with a polite "Thank you." During my stay in Egypt, I always regretted not asking her more directly to help arrange an interview with the President.

Despite my failure to meet her husband, the interview with Madame Sadat was delightful. During the course of our conversation she told me about a few behind-the-scenes incidents of the revolution. In his book, *The Revolt of the Nile*, Sadat states that the uprising by the "young Turks" had been brought forward an hour. Sadat was not informed of this and was watching a movie at the time of the outbreak. Madame Sadat smiled as she told me the story from a slightly different perspective. "Actually he had gone with me to see the movie. When we got back there was a message from someone at my husband's desk. He read it and rushed out again. He didn't say a word to me and it wasn't until the next morning, when I heard the voice of my own husband reading out the first communique of the revolution over the radio, that I knew what had happened. That was the first I had heard of the revolution."

Madame Sadat is a tall, beautiful women, with a little English blood in her. I can see her now as I write, her hair floating in the sea breeze. The place where we had tea was sheltered from the sea by a fence so that it is impossible for anyone to peek into the house from the sea.

Just two miles east of El Mamura lies Abu Qir, the scene of a famous battle. On August 1, 1798, Admiral Nelson of the British fleet, defeated Napoleon's navy after a major sea-battle. This established British naval supremacy. One of the islands along the coast is named Nelson Island in commemoration of the battle and its commander. It was while Napoleon's engineers were stationed forty miles east of Alexandria at Rosetta that they discovered the famous Rosetta Stone in 1799. Today Abu Qir is a tiny fishing village with a fine beach and numerous restaurants which serve delicious and really fresh fish. The village children will come and sell just-caught sea urchins to the guests in the restaurant. In front of their customers the children dexterously open the shells of the sea urchins which are as prickly as hedgehogs. This seafood tastes wonderful and is quite cheap.

Back in the center of Alexandria is the Greco-Roman Museum. This is where I became entranced by the exhibits of beautiful Roman glass. Some of this glass had been buried so long before being discovered that it had turned a silver color and now emits a strange iridescent light. Relics of Roman glass have been found in Lebanon and Syria as well as in Alexandria.

I lost my heart to one piece in particular. I found it in an antique shop next to the St. George Hotel in Beirut, but someone purchased it before I was able to do so. After tracking it for a number of years, I finally heard that it was located in an antique shop in—of all places—my hometown of Tokyo. Upon my return to Japan, I rushed to the shop only to find that once again the piece had eluded me; it had been purchased just a few months before during a department store exhibition. I still feel that my heart belongs to this particular object—rather like an unrequited love—and as a result I have lost interest in all other pieces of glass.

The increased traffic of military and merchant vessels in the harbor has created a noticeable increase in the amount of pollution in the waters off Alexandria. It is said that the waters of the harbor were once so clear that at it was possible to see the remains of the Pharos Lighthouse and its island on the seabed. This may be a folktale, but certainly today the harbor is very polluted. The really good swimming beaches are further west. I once rented a house for the summer at the lovely health resort of Sidi Abdel Rahman. Few people visit this area and it was possible to lie awake at night hearing only the gentle lapping of the waves. The sea, a cobalt blue, washed up on silver-white beach. The area appeared to be untainted by pollution. However, after swimming or walking along the breakwater, I would be surprised to find little black smudges of oil, obviously discharged from ships, on the soles of my feet.

Halfway between this area and Alexandria is the famous battlefield of El Alamein, the scene of fierce fighting in the autumn of 1942 between General Montgomery's British troops and the soldiers of the Axis powers under General Rommel. The Axis powers lost this battle, and casualties on both sides amounted to 30,000. The struggle between these two forces is embodied in the present-day name of the place, the Arabic for "The Two Flags." Under cloudless blue skies and amid the dusty yellow of the desert stretch the carefully tended cemeteries of the British, the Germans and the Italians. The El Alamein War Museum is also here with helmets, pistols, machine guns, flags, maps and the other materiel of the war. Old tanks stand in front of the museum.

A young Egyptian soldier named Wagidi, who showed me around, told me that land mines were still being found in the desert. "A few months ago," he said, "someone stepped on one and was blown up and killed." He went on to tell me that he had only been in the army a year but that he loathed war and wanted to study to become an agricultural engineer.

One of the exhibits I found most interesting. It was a scene reconstructed with life-sized dolls and depicted villagers of the area selling information to Rommel. According to Wagidi, a villager named Ali Heida, who was living in the Siwa Oasis was simultaneously selling information to Rommel and Montgomery. Ali Heida is still alive and occasionally shows up in El Alamein, bewailing his present fate and saying that he really made "quite a killing in the old days."

During the Fourth Middle East War, tank battles more fierce than those in El Alamein took place on the Sinai Peninsula, between Israeli and Egyptian troops. Now, a little on the far side of El Alamein, an oil-drilling platform overlooks the cemeteries of the dead of the last world war. General Montgomery, the victor of El Alamein, received a dukedom from the British crown which carried the formal title of Lord Montgomery of Alamein. But the victor, too, has gone, dying peacefully at the end of a full life on March 24, 1976, at the age of eighty-eight.

122   CAIRO

76–79. The Roman theater of Kom-el-Dikka in the foreground and the modern buildings seen in the background (*preceding page*) present two faces of Alexandria. Founded in 331 B.C., it is today an international city with a population of two million. *Right* and *below*: The Mediterranean glistens alongside the Alexandrian beaches. *Opposite*: Horse-drawn carriages and late-model cars share space on the July 26 Avenue.

80. The vaulted ceiling of the Abu-el-Abbas Mosque is an intricate, intriguing work of art.
81. The Serapeum (*right*) was a temple complex constructed during the Ptolemaic Dynasty. Jutting from the right of the picture is Pompey's Column.

82–85. Alexandrian scenes—fish is a popular food (*below*); the trolley still runs through the city streets (*right*); fabric merchants unfold their goods; a bazaar where fresh fruit is sold (*opposite*).

86. The sun sets majestically on the quiet Mediterranean. 87. *Right*: El Montazah is one of the most popular resorts in Egypt. 88. *Preceding page*: Montazah Palace, which is now a museum and whose gardens are now a public park, was formerly the summer residence of King Farouk.

89. *Below*: The Lighthouse of Pharos was one of the Seven Wonders of the Ancient World. It is said that the beam of its light was visible from five hundred kilometers. 90–92. The Graeco-Roman Museum has an excellent collection which includes artifacts dating to 3000 B.C. This statue of the sacred bull of Apis (*right*) is one of its valuable pieces. *Bottom* and *opposite*: A statuary gallery and the museum's facade.

93–95. *This page*: Scenes of the Nile Delta region—date palms heavy with fruit, the Alexandria–Cairo train, and ripening wheat in the fields. 96. *Opposite*: Cotton accounts for about fifty percent of Egyptian exports. The quality of this cotton is among the highest in the world. 97. *Overleaf*: The Alexandrian coast at dusk.

THIS BEAUTIFUL WORLD

THE HIMALAYAS
PALACES OF KYOTO
PEKING
GODS OF KUMANO
MOSCOW
MICHELANGELO
AFGHANISTAN
HAWAII
SEOUL
GOYA
THE ALPS
THE ACROPOLIS
VIENNA
AFRICAN ANIMALS
THAILAND
YOSEMITE
SAN FRANCISCO
BALI
SPAIN
MEXICO
IMPERIAL VILLAS OF
  KYOTO
JOURNEY THROUGH
  AFRICA
THE GRAND CANYON
CALIFORNIA
MONGOLIA
LAPLAND
THE GREEK ISLANDS
HONG KONG
ANGKOR WAT
ISTANBUL

THE ROAD TO HOLY
  MECCA
BURMA
THE ANDES
NEW GUINEA
MARKETPLACES OF THE
  WORLD
TRADITIONAL TOKYO
IRELAND
AUSTRALIA
INDIA
CHERRY BLOSSOMS
OKINAWA
NEW YORK
LONDON
SRI LANKA
IRAN
YUGOSLAVIA
WASHINGTON
ROME
BRAZIL
ALASKA
DELHI AND AGRA
BOSTON
MALAYSIA
EL SALVADOR
VENICE
ST. LOUIS
PHILIPPINES
CAIRO
FLORIDA
KASHMIR

In preparation

KATMANDU

SWITZERLAND